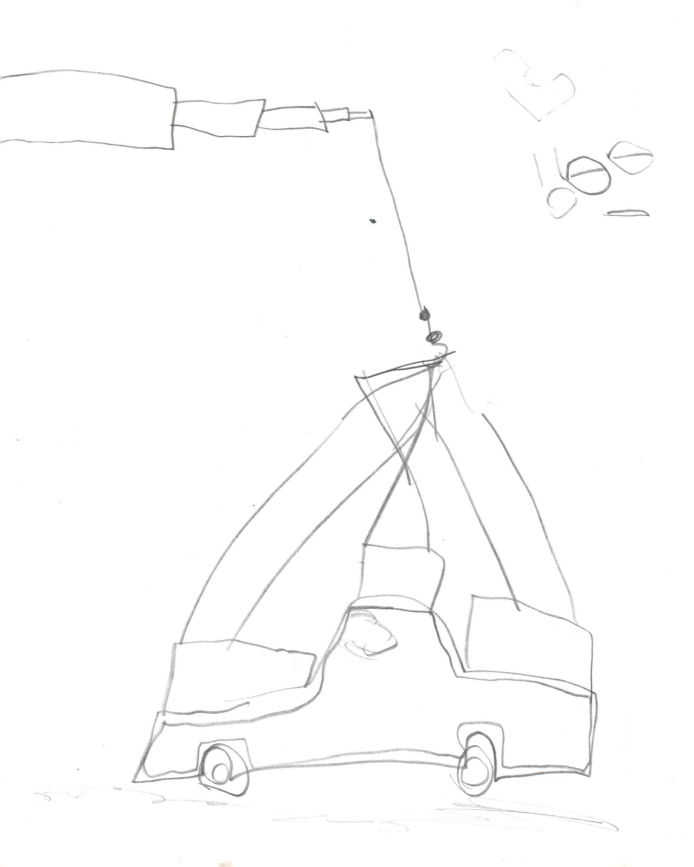

TRIUMPH BOOKS

The **BIG BOOK** Of
MINECRAFT

This book is available in quantity at special discounts for your group or organization.
For further information, contact:

Triumph Books LLC
814 North Franklin Street
Chicago, Illinois 60610
Phone: (312) 337-0747
www.triumphbooks.com

Printed in U.S.A.
ISBN: 978-1-62937-028-6

Content packaged by Mojo Media, Inc.
Joe Funk: Editor
Jason Hinman: Creative Director
Trevor Talley: Writer

Contents

INTRODUCTION

HERE'S YOUR PICKAXE & HELMET

If you've got this book in your hands, you've probably heard a bit about Minecraft. From its origins as a cult game with a small but dedicated following to one of the biggest video games of all time (if not the biggest), Minecraft is truly on a roll. With every passing year, the game gets on new platforms, gets in the hands of new players and, to put it simply, gets more and more massively popular. And there's a good reason for that.

Put simply, Minecraft is one of the most inventive, creative and unique games ever created. Posing as a simple survival and world-building game, Minecraft fans have taken its unique system and caused it to blossom into something much more: a global cultural phenomenon.

In fact, Minecraft's genius has earned it so many fans all over the world, it's now considered one of the most successful games ever released for not one, but three major gaming systems (PC, console and smartphones). To put it in numerical terms: as of summer 2014, the game has sold over 50 million copies on the PC, 54 million copies on the console and 21 million copies on smartphones. Put together, those 125 million copies are just shy of the entire populations of Mexico and Canada put together.

With so many people taking the plunge into the crazy, block-filled world of Minecraft, it's no wonder you might be curious about the game. But like many before you, you might be asking yourself, "What is it about this low-resolution existence that people like so much?"

WHAT IS MINECRAFT?

Let's get this out of the way right off the bat: Minecraft is not like other games.

The basic premise of Minecraft is that you are a character who has spawned into a world that's entirely made up of materials, which you can harvest, and populated by creatures called mobs, which you can kill. Your immediate goal is this: survive.

There are animals and plants for food, and materials to build a shelter, but the world of Minecraft is not all out to help you. At night, hostile, dangerous mobs come out to try their best to kill you and maybe even wreck your home a bit.

Once you've secured your defenses against the dark, dark night, however, the resemblance to a typical video game ends.

Minecraft has little plot, the graphics are basic (though we think they're cool looking) and it rarely tells you what to do next. So why is Minecraft so popular?

From your dream home to pirate boats straight out of history, Minecraft lets your imagination run wild.

MORE THAN SURVIVING

It's simple: Minecraft is whatever you want it to be. That might sound like exaggeration, but it really isn't. Everything you see in the world of Minecraft can be changed, from knocking down a tall mountain, to drying up a lake to building enormous structures that tower into the sky anywhere you like.

This is possible because everything in the environment of Minecraft is created by blocks, each of which is made up of a resource such as Stone or Wood. These blocks can be removed by "breaking" them, and you can then either use them to build the world the way you'd like, or you can turn them into even more materials and items. All it takes is a little exploring, and you can find the resources to create just about anything.

Not only can you create your own worlds in Minecraft...

...but you can also explore the entire universes Crafted by the minds of players all over the globe!

EXPLORE, EXPLORE AND EXPLORE FURTHER

And Minecraft does not shirk or mess about when it comes to giving you plenty to explore. One of the master strokes of this modern classic game is that it uses complex algorithms to create massively diverse and unique worlds to explore every time you load it.

There are endless deserts populated by thriving Villages and cut through with winding rivers. There are towering snowy mountains that cast shadows over sweeping plains dotted with flowers, Lava fields and cave entrances. There are even multiple dimensions and an underground filled with ruins and adventures that will take you dozens of hours to fully explore, if you can survive the creatures that dwell there.

THE REAL REASON MINECRAFT IS GREAT

In the end though, there's one reason Minecraft has cemented its status as a truly great game, and that's this: Minecraft is only limited by your imagination.

If you can think of it, you can build it or make it happen. That is, if you know how the game works.

WHAT YOU'LL FIND IN THE BIG BOOK OF MINECRAFT

What you have in your hands is The Big Book of Minecraft, and it's a whopper. We have now put out two Minecraft guides (Minecrafter and Minecrafter 2.0) to help you with that "knowledge of the game" part of the game, and now we've put together the best of the best from our past two books and thrown in some brand-spanking-new chapters in what is truly the biggest, baddest Minecraft guide yet.

We want you to be the best Minecrafter you can be, and it's a time-honored Minecraft tradition for veteran players to pass down their knowledge to newcomers. Here you'll find everything you need to get started and begin your first monumental creation, but don't get us wrong, this guide isn't just for the noobs.

The Big Book is also full of advanced info, exclusive strategies and tips and tricks that even the best pros will find useful. With chapters that take you from the early stages of the game all the way through to advanced tactics for combat, mining, farming, exploration, Redstone and just about everything else in the game, this book is meant to be your go-to for any question or issue you might have about Minecraft.

All it takes is the game, an idea and a little time to Craft.

Plus, we've scoured the web for the best and brightest new builds and creations to show off in our 100% new gallery, and we've put together a look into some awesome parts of Minecraft even you hardcore Crafters might not be familiar with yet. That's right: The Big Book includes exclusive info on the insane, wide-world of PC mods that let you transform Minecraft into a whole new game, a guide to the immensely popular realm of online Minecraft mini-games and profiles of the coolest, craftiest Minecraft players in the world, all for your reading enjoyment. You won't find this info anywhere else, and it is some of the coolest stuff we've ever seen in any game, not just in Minecraft.

LET'S BUILD

Now, with the goal of surviving the dark night in order to bring staggering creations of beauty and wonder into the digital world, pick up your phone, mouse or console controller, crack open this book and start up a fresh world of Minecraft.

There's a world of infinite imagination and excitement waiting for you just on the other side of this page, so as we say here at the 'Crafter, grab your Pickaxe and let's dig in!

It's time to build.

NOTE: This book is meant to be useful to as many players as is possible. Because of that, it will focus primarily on items, creatures and gameplay that can be found in the console version of Minecraft, as that is the most popular version and everything in the console version can be found in the PC version as well.

GETTING STARTED

So here you are, you've taken the plunge and bought Minecraft. You're staring at that menu screen, and you're ready to dive into this crazy world you've heard so much about.

Now, you could start up a new world and try and wing it, but trust us, that path leads to darkness (literally), frustration and, yes, death. Minecraft is a game that's at once very simple on the surface and incredibly complex underneath, and what you do when you first

start out can make a huge difference in your success at crafting the world you want. That, plus it's really not much fun to die in the dark from your fourth Creeper attack in a row and lose all of your gear over and over.

To get the most out of Minecraft, you'll have a much better and less death-filled time if you know a few things about the game before jumping right in.

You're seconds from your first game of Minecraft.

THE MENUS

It only takes the push of a few buttons to start up a new Minecraft world, but the good folks at Mojang packed the Minecraft menus full of options that can make a big difference in your overall experience. Of particular importance are the "Help & Options" area and, of course, the "Play Game" button.

HELP & OPTIONS

The title says it all—this is where you want to go to find everything from audio and visual settings to new skins for your avatar and mini-guides on how to deal with certain aspects of the game. Much of this can be accessed in-game, so it's not entirely necessary that you look through this or tweak it in any way until you've played a little, but it's good to know that it's there ahead of time.

PLAY GAME

This is where the magic happens. The "Play Game" button is what kicks off your Minecraft experience, whether it's starting a new world with "Create New World," trying out the "Tutorial" or getting back into one of the games you've already begun. As you'll see, when you open the "Play Game" menu for the first time, you only have the option to start a new world up or to give the built-in tutorial a try, but later any worlds you start and save will show up here.

You start with nothing in Minecraft.

And there are things that want to kill you right off the bat.

HOW TO START A GAME

Ready to start a world?! Select "Create New World" from the "Play Game" menu, and take a gander at all the options you've got! Here's a big not-so-secret about Minecraft: there are just about an infinite number of possible worlds to try out, and not all are created equal. In fact, you'll find new environments that require different tactics in almost every world you start, which is one of the reasons Minecraft is such a popular game.

When preparing a world for play, you've got two sets of options to look at.

Make your selections.

THE PRIMARY OPTIONS

These are the most important options for making your new world just how you want it, and they're the only ones you actually have to set. The first three, "Online Game," "Invite Only" and "Allow Friends of Friends" all have to do with playing single player or multiplayer. You can start a game by yourself no matter which of these are checked, but if you want other people to play with you, make sure "Online Game" is checked and then check the other two depending on who you want to be able to join.

"World Name" isn't too important, but it is what your world will be permanently saved as, so pick something memorable!

"Seed for the World Generator," however, is very important to how your world comes out. Seeds are numbers that the game uses to create your world, and they can either be set manually (if you want to play a seed you've heard about) or left blank for a random seed based on the time.

You'll now need to set the type of game you're playing. For the console version, this means choosing between "Creative" or "Survival" modes and the two are exactly what they sound like. "Creative" mode is all about making things, and you get access to every single item and material in the game without having to find them. Additionally, you can fly and manipulate the world however you want. "Survival" mode, on the other hand, forces you to find and/or create items and structures from what's in the world around you, and all the while you'll be fighting against hostile monsters and the elements. This guide is mostly centered on "Survival" mode, though "Creative" mode is absolutely worth checking out too.

Finally, you need to set a difficulty level, for which you have four options:

Peaceful: No hostile mobs exist. You don't need to eat.

Easy: Hostile mobs are fewer and do less damage. Not eating does less damage.

In Creative Mode you have access to every item and material in the game.

Normal: The standard number of mobs spawn and do standard damage. Not eating depletes your health.

Hard: There are more monsters and they will seriously mess you up if they catch you, and not eating can kill you.

For your first game, we suggest trying either "Normal" or "Easy."

Here's where you can tweak the game a bit more.

MORE OPTIONS

The "More Options" button lets you tweak your world a little more, though you can leave it alone if you want. Here you'll find eight more options to turn on or off, and these fall into the following categories:

Online Game Options: "Player vs Player" lets you decide whether multiplayer participants can hurt each other or not, while "Trust Players" is an option you can turn off if you don't want newcomers to be able to build or destroy until you say so. "Host Privileges" turns on the option for you, the host of the game, to have special abilities if you want them, but it also negates any achievements you get from playing.

You're just a few menus away from your first mine.

The world that awaits you.

Craft with a friend!

Fire and TnT: Turn these off if you want fire and TNT to do no damage.

World Options: If "Generate Structures" is turned off, you won't find any Villages, Nether Forts or Strongholds in your game, each of which is a structure you can find out more about in the "Navigating Villages and Structures" section of the guide. "Superflat World" makes everything flat, just like it sounds. "Bonus Chest" can make a big difference to how your first few days go. It spawns a chest near your starting point that contains quite a few usable items, meaning you don't have to make your own.

Using the above info, make your menu choices the way you'd like them to be, and then press "Create New World" to start up your very first world!

CONTROLLING YOUR MINER

Minecraft controls are pretty darn simple, and if you've ever played a First Person Shooter game, you're already familiar with the basic idea. For those that haven't, your RS (right stick) looks around the world, while the LS (left stick) moves you forward, backward and in any other direction in a straight line without changing which direction you're looking.

You're seconds from your first game of Minecraft.

The lettered buttons on the right of your controller (X, Y, B and A) control Crafting, Inventory, Throw Item and Jump, respectively, while LB (left button) and RB (right button) cycle through items in your inventory tray at the bottom of your screen. Two of the most important buttons are LT (left trigger), which opens menus for Crafting Tables, Furnaces and other crafting mechanisms and eats food, and RT (right trigger), which uses the item in your hand to hit blocks and triggers mechanisms like buttons.

YOUR FIRST FEW MINUTES

Right, so you're in the world of Minecraft. You've got no items, no shelter and a whole wide world out there to explore. But what to do first? While you can really do whatever you want, if you want to survive your first day (and night!), you should do two things: look around, and gather resources.

This is a great starting location between two Biomes.

A simple spawn point beacon.

LOOKING AROUND

When starting a new game, the first thing to do is put a marker down where you started. To do this, dig out some Dirt from the ground with your hand and stack it in a column. This will help a lot later. Now, simply look around a bit and see where you've started. Minecraft is split up into different environments called "Biomes," and each Biome contains specific plants, animals, resources and terrain-types. You can build and mine in any Biome, but some are much more convenient and safe when it comes to creating a shelter to live in. The number one priority is trees, because without trees, you aren't going to be able to craft important tools and items. After that, look for areas with Water, animals and easily defendable terrain such as mountaintops. One good trick is to find a spot where two Biomes meet and build there. Remember though: nighttime comes fast, so don't spend too much time traveling on your first day.

GATHERING RESOURCES

On your first day out, you want to make every second count, so while you're looking for a nice place to set up a shelter, you'll need to be gathering resources. At the beginning of the game, certain resources are more important than others. The smartest order for gathering goes Wood>Cobblestone>Food>Wool, but if something is very close to you (say a Pig wanders by), take the opportunity to pick it up.

To gather Wood, you need to punch some trees. The noble art of tree-punching is what starts just about every game of Minecraft, and to do this, point the crosshairs at the wood of the trunk and punch the blocks until they break. This is the slowest way of collecting Wood, however, and you'll want an Axe as soon as possible.

You're just a few menus away from your first mine.

When you've collected at least 3 Wood, open your crafting menu and create a set of four Wood Planks, then create a Crafting Table. The recipe for the Crafting Table is one block of Wood Planks in each of the four squares of the menu. You can then place your crafting table anywhere in the environment. Now, to make an Axe, point at your Crafting Table after you place it and open the Crafting Table menu. You should then turn all of your remaining Wood into Wood Planks and turn at least 2 of your new Wood Planks into Sticks. Once you have at least 3 Wood Planks and 2 Sticks, you can create your first tool, an Axe!

Your first shelter should be simple and effective.

BUILDING A SHELTER

With your Axe, you can now chop down trees much quicker. Continue doing this until you have about 30-40 Wood (you may need to create another Axe if yours breaks), then break up your Crafting Table by chopping it, pick it up and move to where you want to build a house.

Place your Crafting Table and turn about 2/3 of your Wood into Wood Planks (you need about 60-100). Put the Wood Planks in your inventory tray, and start building a house! The quickest way to do this is to create a rectangular shelter at least 4 blocks long, 2 blocks wide and 4 blocks tall. Build the bottom layer first, then jump on top and run around it putting up the second layer. Repeat for the third and fourth layers, and then jump in.

A good first shelter.

Doors are a necessity. You don't want those Creepers sneakin' in!

Before you fill in the hole with a ceiling, you need light, and light means Torches. Torches are created with one Stick and one Coal or Charcoal. To get Coal, you have to find a Coal deposit and mine it with a Pickaxe, and to get Charcoal, you need to burn Wood in a Furnace, which means you need to gather Cobblestone.

Wooden Pickaxe.

Soon enough, you'll be able to knock out a neat little mine like this one.

GATHERING MORE RESOURCES

At this point, you need to build your first Pickaxe, the most famous and useful tool in the game! To do this, open your Crafting Table menu up again and create the Wooden Pickaxe (you may need to make more Wood Planks and Sticks to do this).

With your trusty new Wooden Pickaxe, you are now able to mine your first Stone (a big moment!). Leave your house by chopping a hole 2 blocks high and 1 block wide in the wall, and look around where you are. Try to find a hill or mountainside with exposed Stone. If you can't see any, you can just pick a spot and dig down until you hit some. Remember to leave a few blocks that you can jump on to get out.

At this point, you need at least 8 Cobblestone, but gathering around 20-30 won't hurt if you have time. Once you have some Cobblestone, head back to your shelter.

A shelter that's ready for night.

It won't take long before your simple home starts to look like a mighty dwelling.

Before you build a Furnace, let's put a door on that home. Open your Crafting Table, and create the Wooden Door (this takes some Planks). Step outside your home again, select the door in your Inventory Tray and point your crosshairs at the hole in the side of your shelter. Use the Left Trigger to place the door, then open it and walk in.

Go to your Crafting Table again and move to the Chest icon. Push down on the D-Pad, and then create the Furnace when it shows up. Place the Furnace anywhere in your shelter, and then open it up with Left Trigger. Furnaces take fuel, which is something burnable like Wood or Coal. Put some of your remaining Wood in the top item slot, and then use Wood, Wood Planks or something else made of Wood in the bottom one. You'll see the Furnace come on as it starts to turn your Wood into Charcoal.

While this is happening, finish the roof to your home. Make sure it's fully enclosed, or else a Spider could fall on your head during the night!

Now, check your Furnace. Take the Charcoal from the Furnace, and open your Crafting Table back up. In the Tools section, you'll see Torches. Use all of your Charcoal up making Torches, and then start placing your Torches on the walls and ground around your home.

Once you've got a completed shelter, you can continue gathering resources until Nighttime. Soon enough, you'll start seeing the sun go down, which means Nighttime is about to arrive with all of its terrors. But no worries, because you've got a handy little shelter to protect you! Congrats on your first day in Minecraft.

NIGHTTIME

Here's the deal: when night falls on the world of Minecraft, things are going to try and kill you. A lot. All night long. This is because the monsters in Minecraft, known as "hostile mobs," can only survive when the level of light is low (except for Slimes, Spiders and the dreaded Creeper, which can survive in the day). Add that to the fact that hostile mobs spawn randomly at Nighttime and then attack you on sight, and you've got yourself a bit of a dangerous situation for your character.

To put it simply, when that sun goes down, you had better be prepared to deal with the perils of night until that blissful moment when you see the light start to peek back over the horizon. If you're not prepared, you can be sure that your character is not going to survive.

So, what can you do to protect yourself in the dark, dangerous Minecraft Nighttime? Luckily, you've got quite a few options, and you should have no problem keeping safe and snug with even the most basic preparation during the day.

This situation is very easy to fall into at night.

THE NECESSITIES

You need two things for certain if you're going to live to see another day in Minecraft: Shelter and Lighting.

SHELTER

The Primary Number One Super Important Thing to have that will keep you safe from all of the Zombies, Skeletons, Endermen, Spiders and (shudder) Creepers at night is a nice shelter. You can read all the details on how to build a good basic shelter in the "Getting Started/Your First Day" section of this guide, but the basic idea is that you need an enclosed area with no open spaces to hide in. That's actually all you need to stay safe at night, but it'll be a dark, boring Nighttime without at least a little light.

LIGHTING

Torches are your best friend in Minecraft, and you definitely need some in your shelter. Again, check out the "Getting Started/Your First Day" section to see exactly how to make a few Torches. Another way Torches are super useful at night besides letting you see (which is pretty darn useful, we'd say) is to keep monsters from spawning. Light in Minecraft is measured on a scale of 1-15, and monsters cannot spawn in any light level above 7. By placing Torches in an area, you can keep monsters from spawning there, though they can still travel through it. To do this, you need to put torches so that there are no more than 11 blocks between them in a straight line and no more than 5 between them diagonally.

After you've built the basic base, it's time to start decorating and filling it with awesome stuff!

THE SECONDARY IDEAS

While you don't absolutely need these things, your Nighttime experience will be a heck of a lot safer and more fun if you have them.

A BED

This is the most useful tool to have at night, and it's one of the first things you should try and build in Minecraft. A Bed is a 2 block long item that can be placed in your world and slept in during the night, which instantly makes it day again. Not only that, but sleeping in a Bed sets your spawn point to that bed, meaning that when you die, you won't have to run back to your shelter!

To build a Bed takes 3 Wood Planks and 3 Wool of any color. Wool is relatively easy to come by, as it drops when you kill Sheep. Use your Crafting Table to combine the Wood Planks and Wool, and set your Bed someplace where the sides are unobstructed. Then, just sleep in it when it's Nighttime, and you'll skip right through the danger to daytime.

A nicely lit room.

Everyone needs a bed!

WEAPONS & ARMOR

When you start a game in Minecraft, you're basically an unprotected weakling. Sad to say, but it's true. That doesn't have to remain the case though, as you can beef up your character's power through crafting weapons and armor to use in combat.

Basic weapons are easy to get early on, as you only need 1 Stick and 2 Wood Planks or Cobblestone to make a Sword. Do this as soon as you can, as it makes a huge difference in your attack and will often save your life during combat. In fact, even a Wooden Sword does four times the damage that punching does, and that damage rating goes up with better materials (except Gold).

Other weapons in Minecraft include Bows, Tools and Potions, each of which does differing amounts of damage, with Tools being the least effective. You can also use other items in the game, such as Cobwebs, Cactus, Snowballs, Fishing Rods and Buckets of Water or lava to hinder or damage mobs in various ways, so get creative!

Armor, unlike weapons, can take a while to create because it requires a large amount of rare materials. Basic armor is made of Leather (dropped from a killed Cow), while better armor is crafted of Iron or Diamond (you can also use Gold, but this is not effective or recommended). Armor is worth making once you have enough Leather or a few extra Iron, as it makes an enormous difference in the amount of damage you can take.

With weapons and armor handy, you can actually brave the Nighttime a little, though your chances at dying are still pretty high.

SOMETHING TO DO

Once you've got a Bed, you don't need to deal with the night, but having to return to your Bed to sleep can get annoying after a while, especially if you're playing multiplayer (players must sleep at the same time). Because of that, it can be useful and fun to take the Nighttime as a chance to do a few things.

A Crafter fully decked out in armor and weapons.

On the attack!

The most obvious thing to do at night is to work on the inside of your shelter! Whether you decorate it, reorganize your materials, build more Crafting Tables, Furnaces or other useful items or even create another room or story, this is a great time to do this.

Nighttime is also a good time to refine your materials, such as making Iron Ingots out of Iron Ore or creating some extra tools. Use your extra few minutes and get some stuff made!

Another great idea is to create a mineshaft that's accessible through your own home. You'll want to make sure this has a door on it to keep out mobs, but this can be an easy and efficient way to mine for resources while staying relatively safe.

Finally, once you're pretty confident in your weapons, armor and combat skills, you can go monster hunting at night...if you dare. Most mobs drop useful items when killed, and a small excursion out to hunt monsters can be very rewarding.

Some mobs burn during the day!

A few walls and some Torches are all you need.

NIGHTTIME FACTS

Here are a few facts about Nighttime that can help you out:

Nighttime lasts 7 minutes of real time

Sunset/dusk is a short period of 1½ minutes real time during which players can go to sleep

Light decreases by 1 every 10 seconds during dusk

The natural light level at Nighttime is 4

Crops can still grow at night

Sleeping through night, however, essentially stops time, so no crops grow and Furnaces pick up where they left off when you went to sleep

The day/night cycle continues even when you're in The Nether or The End

Spiders, Creepers and Slime are the only hostile mobs that do not die in the daylight

A random song will start to play at the beginning of each cycle of time

A pair of towers sits atop an Extreme Hills Biome.

BIOMES

What exactly do we mean by "Biomes"?
This might seem like an easy question to answer, and in a basic sense, the definition of "Biome" in Minecraft is pretty straightforward: Biomes are the different types of land you can find in Minecraft. However, there are actually two distinct types of Biomes that can be found in the game. For this book, we'll call them "Area Biomes" and "Feature Biomes," respectively, and you'll notice when you play that you'll often find them existing together, with the Feature Biome set within the larger Area Biome.

Area Biomes: We use this term in Minecrafter to refer to the large sections of land that contain certain plants, mobs and aesthetics (for instance, Desert Biomes are mostly yellow and tan with little life, while the Jungle Biome is lush with life and is full of deep greens and browns). When running around the world of Minecraft, Area Biomes are what you'll most often be in when above ground, and the border between one Area Biome and the next is usually pretty easy to see, as the ground will change color from one Biome to the next. Think of Area Biomes as different types of nature, or environments.

Feature Biomes: Where Area Biomes refer to areas where certain plants and mobs live, Feature Biomes are more recognizable by their shape. Think of them as natural structures, including Beaches, Rivers, Ravines and Hills. Caves aren't technically considered a Biome, but we've included them with Feature Biomes as they have many similarities.

WHY YOU SHOULD KNOW YOUR BIOMES

Other than the obvious reason that you want to be an ultra-level, super-guru, Minecrafter genius-person, there is an important practical reason that knowing your various Biomes is a great idea: some items, mobs, structures and even Feature Biomes exist mostly or even exclusively in specific Biomes.

For instance, say you're looking for a lot of Wood and you need it really quickly. Well, if you know your Biomes, you know to stay away from the Desert Biome, and hopefully there's a Jungle Biome nearby. Ready to go cave-diving? The Extreme Hills Biome is your best bet, and you're unlikely to find what you're looking for in the Jungle.

The fact that not all Biomes are created equal, and that some contain resources you'll need more often (like Wood) and others don't, also makes it important to know Biomes at the beginning of your game when choosing a spot for a home. There's nothing worse than building a super-sweet house and then realizing that you'll have to hoof it about five minutes to the north to get more Wood because you built your home in a Biome without many trees.

THE BIOME BREAKDOWN

So now that you know why you'll be an even better Crafter when you get your Biome game on lockdown, let's get into it! While we're not going to get into the crazy math that goes behind each Biome (it's out there online, if you're interested), we are going to give you a basic idea of what each Biome is like, what you can find there, why you might want to visit it and whether or not it's a good spot to build a base. We've simplified the info for the Feature Biomes, as they are more about looks and things don't spawn exclusively in them.

PLAINS BIOME:

What It's Like: One of the more common Biomes, the Plains (or Grasslands) is full of Grass, Flowers and some smaller trees. It usually features plenty of mobs (both hostile and friendly) roaming about, and you can sometimes find caves, lakes, Villages and Lava pools scattered around it.

Unique Items, Resources and Mobs: None

Reasons to Visit: It's peaceful and has plentiful Grass (for Seeds) and peaceful mobs to hunt. It's also good for later in the game when you have a lot of resources and want a big space to build something in.

Good for a Base? Only on the edges. Building too far into the Plains will lead to lots of time spent running to Forest Biomes and others with more resources, but building on the edges of the Plains can be fun.

FOREST BIOME

What It's Like: Trees, trees and more Trees! Another very common Biome, the Forest Biome is one of the most useful early in the game, as they provide large amounts of Wood.

Unique Items, Resources and Mobs:

· Wolves are often found wandering outside of Forest Biomes, but they tend to spawn here.

· Though you can find plenty of trees elsewhere, the Jungle Biome is the only Biome with a greater concentration of trees (and those are almost exclusively Jungle Trees).

Reasons to Visit: You need Wood! Also, they are excellent for mob hunting, even in the day, as the shadows created by trees are ideal for keeping hostile mobs spawned.

Good for a Base? Absolutely! The easy access to Wood makes Forests great for your first base, though you might want to find an edge of the Forest so that you don't have to clear out so many leaves.

DESERT BIOME

What It's Like: Sparse of life and resources, the Desert is pretty cool-looking, but is not a great place to spend large amounts of time unless it is near another, more resource-heavy Biome.

Unique Items, Resources and Mobs:

· Cactus grows in the Desert and can be used for traps and decoration.

· Sand and Sandstone, while not exclusive to the Desert, will be found in the largest amounts here.

· Dry Bushes also grow here and are mostly used for decoration.

Reasons to Visit: The three primary reasons people head to the Desert are Sand, Cactus and Desert Villages. For whatever reason, Villagers love the Desert, and you'll often find a Village or two within. Primarily, however, Deserts are best for grabbing Sand for making Glass and Sandstone.

Good for a Base? Only at the edge of the Desert and another Biome. It's good to have a Desert near your base (as you'll probably want Glass at some point), but its utter lack of trees is a huge drawback for building a base there.

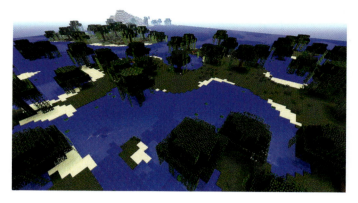

SWAMP BIOME

What It's Like: Lots of little bits of land surrounded by Water. Features short Oak Trees covered in Vines, and often has Mushrooms and Lily Pads around.

Unique Items, Resources and Mobs:
· Lily Pads are most commonly found here. These are fun decorations, but you can also build bridges across Water with them.

Reasons to Visit: Swamps are okay for Wood, but you're always better off finding a Forest Biome when you need large amounts. Most of the reason players go to Swamps is to find the resources that are common there, such as Lily Pads, Vines and Mushrooms.

Good for a Base? Can be a cool-looking spot for your home, but you'll need to have a Forest nearby in the long-run.

EXTREME HILLS BIOME

What It's Like: You'll know this one when you see it: huge hills with massive cliffs, overhangs and even waterfalls. One of the most interesting-looking Biomes there is, and a fan-favorite.

Unique Items, Resources and Mobs: None as of now (Emerald Ore is exclusive here but not yet included on the console versions of Minecraft).

Reasons to Visit: When looking for Caves and resources, this is by far your best bet. Extreme Hills Biomes are absolutely riddled with Cave openings, and because there's so much exposed rock, you'll often be able to simply look around outside for Coal and Iron Ore.

Good for a Base? Again, yes, but only if there's a Forest nearby. One trick is to start at a Forest, collecting a lot of Wood and Saplings, and then move to a nearby Extreme Hills Biome to build your home. As they're great for caves, it helps you later in the game, and you can always plant your Saplings on the Extreme Hills (which looks awesome too).

MUSHROOM ISLAND BIOME

What It's Like: Maybe the most unique Biome, this features purple-ish Mycelium as its primary building block and has Huge Mushrooms that look like trees. Always found out in the Ocean Biome.

Unique Items, Resources and Mobs:

· Mycelium, a unique Dirt-like building block that is purple/grey and which Mushrooms like to grow on.

· Mooshrooms hang out on the Mushroom Island. These are Cows that have Mushrooms growing on them. These are great food sources, as you can get Milk, Beef, Mushrooms and Mushroom Stew from them, as well as Leather.

· Giant Mushrooms are another great food source, as chopping them down gives you large amounts of Mushrooms.

Reasons to Visit: For one, there are no hostile mobs on these islands, so they're nice as sanctuaries. They're also very good for food, and if you can manage to get a Mooshroom back to your base, you'll have a constant plentiful food source.

Good for a Base? Nope. You could always build a secondary base on one, or a bridge or tunnel connecting your base to one, but because they are so isolated out in the Water, you're going to constantly have to go back to the main landmass to get other resources.

TAIGA BIOME

What It's Like: Can often be snowy and is a sort-of "Russian"-style forest with Spruce Trees and Wolves.

Unique Items, Resources and Mobs:

· Another great place to find Wolves (though again, they aren't unique to here).

· The best bet for Spruce Trees.

Reasons to Visit: Mostly just to chop down Spruce Trees or find Wolves to tame.

Good for a Base? Can be, though you'll be stuck with just one Wood type for the most part. Mostly good for raiding for Spruce Wood.

JUNGLE BIOME

What It's Like: BIIIIIG trees. Like, really, really big trees. And lots of them. Tons of foliage in general, and usually some hilly areas and lakes.

Unique Items, Resources and Mobs:

· Jungle Trees. These are absolutely the best Wood resource out there, and you'll love finding a Jungle just to get at these giant trees. They can be as big as four times wider than a normal Tree and many, many times taller. You'll often find them covered in Vines as well.

· Cocoa Pods are sometimes found on Jungle trees and are used in food crafting.

· Ocelots! One of the cutest and most useful mobs, the Ocelot is very hard to catch but when tamed they can be used as pets or as guards against Creepers (that's right, Creepers hate Cats and won't go near 'em!)

Reasons to Visit: Get on top of Jungle Tree and chop down all the Wood you'll ever need (well, for about a project or so at least). You'll also want Cats at some point to protect your stuff, so Ocelot taming is a good reason as well.

Good for a Base? Sure! With all that Wood around, why not try a tree-house? You'll probably need to visit others for certain resources, but the Jungle is a great Biome for building, if you can clear out a spot.

OCEAN BIOME

What It's Like: Lots and lots of Water, going off into the distance. There are also underwater Caves and Squids!

Unique Items, Resources and Mobs:

· Squids can sometimes find their ways into Rivers, but you're mostly gonna find these neat little guys (that drop Ink Sacs) in the Ocean.

Reasons to Visit: If you're feeling adventurous and want to try an underwater cave, or if you need a Squid. They can also be pretty good for taking a Boat around, as you can explore the coast.

Good for a Base? Not at all. The Ocean has zero Wood and is hard to build in, not to mention breathe. Of course, everyone wants to have an underwater base at some point, so if you've got the resources, it's a fun place for a secondary home later in the game.

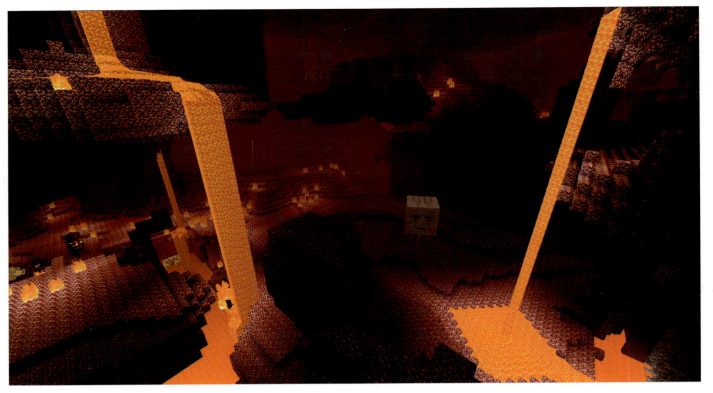

NETHER BIOME

What It's Like: Fire, Lava, things trying to kill you constantly, little in the way of food. Basically super, super hostile.

Unique Items, Resources and Mobs:
TONS. The Nether is like a whole new world, and most of what you'll find there is exclusive.

- Nether Rack is a red building block that when set on fire stays on fire.

- Nether Brick is made from Nether Rack and has a similar relationship to Stone's relationship to Cobblestone.

- Soul Sand is a building block that makes things move slow, great for docks for your Boat.

- Glowstone is a building block that produces light.

- Nether Wart is a plant resource that is used in recipes and only found in the Nether.

- Magma Cubes are like Slimes, but made of fire and Lava and are pretty darn dangerous.

- Ghasts are huge, flying creatures that shoot fireballs and will seriously mess you up.

- Zombie Pigmen are passive, unless you attack them, and they wield weapons.

- Blazes are some of the more dangerous mobs, floating around and shooting Fire Charges at you.

You'll need to kill some at some point if you want to make it to The End.

Reasons to Visit: Besides all of the unique resources, the mobs and the unique things they drop, you'll need to get to the Nether to get items you need to get to The End.

Good for a Base? You can try, but Beds explode on placement in the Nether, so don't expect to get too comfy. Take Stone and Cobblestone with you, as you're going to need something to protect you from Ghast blasts.

FEATURE BIOMES

RIVER BIOME

What It's Like: Neat little rivers, cutting through the land and giving it definition.

Reasons to Visit: They look very cool, and it's always fun to build near one.

RAVINE BIOME

What It's Like: Giant gashes cut into the land that go down very, very far. These can be on the surface or underground, and can often contain waterfalls and Lava falls.

Reasons to Visit: They can be neat to build across or on either side of, but mostly they are just spectacular for getting ore and finding caves, as you can just look at the wall and see where the deposits are.

HILLS BIOME

What It's Like: Just plain ole hills, these can occur on many Biomes including Desert, Plains and Forests.

Reasons to Visit: Good for building on top of, as they offer a view of the surrounding mobs at night.

BEACH BIOME

What It's Like: Little bits of Sand on the edge of Water.

Reasons to Visit: Mostly just for Sand, and sometimes they have Clay as well!

FEATURE BIOMES

CAVE BIOME

What It's Like: Winding, often-complex tunnels through the ground, full of hostile mobs.

Reasons to Visit: These are your best-bet for running into the best resources and structures in the game (like Diamond, Redstone, Fortresses and Abandoned Mineshafts). You'll be spending a lot of time in caves, and it's a good idea to find one very big one and build a little base in it to explore from.

"SNOWY" BIOMES

What It's Like: Many Biomes have "cold" or "Snowy" versions where you can find Ice and Snow, as well as get actual snow-falling animations. Plains, Taiga, Rivers and Beaches can all have "Snowy" versions.

Reasons to Visit: You can get Snowballs here, which can be turned into Snow Blocks. Ice is also fun to use, as you slip across it, and the "Snowy" Biomes just look plain awesome.

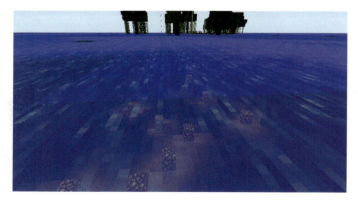

DEEP OCEAN BIOME

What It's Like: The Ocean Biome, except with massive underwater mountains and Ravines.

Reasons to Visit: Same as the Ocean Biome, but good for giant underwater structures.

A Jungle Biome sits just above a Cave Biome, giving this area a quite cool look.

"Infinite power just isn't very interesting, no matter what game you're playing. It's much more fun when you have a limited tool set to use against the odds. Usually, a new player to Minecraft doesn't make it through the first night. They're just not prepared for the danger. It's a harsh lesson but it establishes the rules."

— Notch on why Minecraft is the way it is

MATERIALS

Materials are everything in Minecraft, and we mean that quite literally. Except for player characters, NPCs (Non Player Characters, such as animals and mobs) and a few rare objects, everything you see in Minecraft is either a material or can be made with materials. This is what makes Minecraft so awesome: since everything breaks down into materials, you can destroy and build just about anything you want in the world.

This section of the guide will give you a quick look at the most important materials in the game, as well as a look at what you can make with them. Play enough Minecraft, and you'll come to know each and every one of these materials by heart. You'll know 'em, you'll learn to love 'em (or hate 'em—we're looking at you, Gravel) and soon enough you'll be squealing with glee every time you stumble on some precious, precious Diamond just like the rest of us.

BUILDING BLOCKS

These are what the world of Minecraft is made up of, and they're what you'll mine and harvest to use in your own creations.

DIRT
Found: Overworld almost everywhere
Used In: Early shelters, farming
Best Tool to Use: Shovel

Look around you in the Overworld, and there's probably some Dirt. Dirt is one of the most common blocks, but it's only real uses are for aesthetics and farming. You can make a shelter of it in a pinch, but it's always recommended to use something more stable (and better looking!) when you can. However, Dirt can have things grow on it, including "natural" materials like Snow, Mycelium and Grass as well as farmable materials like trees and Wheat.

WOOD

Types: Oak, Spruce, Birch
Found: Overworld in most Biomes except Desert, Plains and Mushroom
Used In: Wood Planks, which are needed for many items including tools and building materials
Best Tool to Use: Axe

Wood is without a doubt the most important resource in the game for one major reason: you need it to build tools. You also need it for many other items, but without tools, you're not going to be able to do much in Minecraft. You can find Wood just by looking around most worlds.

STONE

Types: Cobblestone, Stone
Found: Overworld, especially underground
Used In: Stone, Stone Bricks, other Stone building materials such as Walls, Furnace, Stone tools, mechanisms
Best Tool to Use: Pickaxe

If you play Minecraft at all, you're going to end up with a whole lot of stone in the form of Cobblestone. Much of the Minecraft world, especially underground, is made of Stone or Cobblestone, both of which drop Cobblestone when mined. This stuff is required to craft a huge number of items, and you'll definitely want to keep a large stock of Stone tools on hand, as they're the easiest advanced tool to craft. They're the easiest advanced tool to craft.

GRAVEL

Found: Overworld everywhere, usually between Stone and Dirt
Used In: Traps and nothing else. It is evil.
Best Tool to Use: Shovel
Drops: Flint

Gravel is evil. We say this because it's basically just there for variety and to make digging a bit more challenging. It's one of the only two blocks that drops when there's not a block below it (the other is Sand), and it can cause damage when falling far enough and can suffocate creatures it falls on that can't get out. Because of this, it's used in traps. It's only other useful feature is that it drops Flint, used in Flint and Steel.

SAND

Types: Sand, Sandstone
Found: Overworld nearWater and in Deserts
Used In: Glass, Sandstone, Sandstone Brick
Best Tool to Use: Pickaxe

Sand is the other block that, like Gravel, falls when there's nothing supporting it. Sand is the base block, from which Sandstone can be crafted, but you can also find naturally occurring Sandstone. Unlike Stone, Sandstone actually drops a Sandstone block when broken with a Pickaxe. Sand is mostly useful for making Sandstone to build with and Glass, which is also needed for Glass Panes.

CLAY

Found: Overworld in
Water, usually in groups. Rare.
Used In: Clay Block, Bricks
Best Tool to Use: Shovel

Perhaps the rarest construction material block out
there, Clay is found in Water mixed up with Sand and
Sandstone blocks, but is much less common than
either of those. Clay is only used in two things: Clay
Blocks and Bricks. Bricks can make a Bricks block,
which is one of the more rarely seen building materials,
as it takes a lot of Clay to get enough to make much.

OBSIDIAN

Found: Overworld where
running Water has met
standing Lava, The End
Used In: Nether Portal,
building shelter, Enchantment Table
Best Tool to Use: Diamond Pickaxe
(nothing else works)

Obsidian is one tough material. In fact, you can only
mine it with a Diamond Pickaxe, and its resistance
level is 6000 (compare to Cobblestone's 30). That
makes Obsidian hard to get, but it's necessary if trying
to build a portal to the Nether or an Enchantment
Table. You can find Obsidian only where running Water
has hit still Lava, or you can create it by pouring Water
over Lava. Because of its high resistance to damage,
Obsidian makes for good safe rooms and walls.

NETHERRACK

Found: The Nether, all over
Used In: Nether Brick, can be
lit on fire indefinitely
Best Tool to Use: hand,
Pickaxe or Golden Pickaxe

This is what the Nether is made of, literally. It's
incredibly quick to mine and is plentiful, which is nice
if you like the way Nether Brick materials look. It has
a very, very low damage resistance and can only be
turned into Nether Brick, however, so it's not exactly
the ideal for most players. Netherrack's ability to be lit
on fire indefinitely makes it a common choice for traps
and fireplaces.

GLOWSTONE

Found: The Nether
Used In: Lighting
Drops: Glowstone Dust
Best Tool to Use: Any

A special block from the Nether, Glowstone is the best
source of light in the game (level 15, Torches are 14). To
get it, you'll have to break some Glowstone blocks and
collect the Glowstone Dust that drops. This can then
be converted back into Glowstone at a Crafting Table.

SOUL SAND

Found: The Nether, often near large Lava lakes

Used In: Traps and slowing mechanisms

Best Tool to Use: Shovel

Soul Sand is another unique Nether block that isn't used for much as of yet. Soul Sand's primary feature is that it slows down any creature that moves across it (items as well), making it useful in traps and mechanisms where slowing is desired. Its slowness effect is compounded when used in conjunction with Water or Ice.

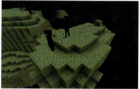

END STONE

Found: The End

Used In: protection from the Ender Dragon

Best Tool to Use: Pickaxe

Another rarely seen block, End Stone is only found in The End, and its main use is as a building material when fighting the Ender Dragon. The Ender Dragon's attack can't destroy End Stone like it can other blocks, but End Stone is a lot easier to mine than Obsidian, making it the best choice for protective shelter in The End.

ORES/MINERALS

When we're talking about the "mining" part of Minecraft, these are the things you'll be looking to find, for the most part. All ores and minerals form in "veins," or pockets that are usually surrounded by Stone, Dirt and Gravel (though sometimes Water and Lava too). They are much harder to find than most blocks, and they are used in most of the complex or advanced creations.

Note: You can craft solid blocks of each of the ores and minerals for use in decoration or certain recipes.

COAL

Types: Charcoal, Coal

Found: Charcoal—Burn Wood in a Furnace, Coal—the Overworld in formations at any level (1% of Stone blocks are Coal)

Used In: Torches, smelting, Fire Charge, running Powered Minecarts

Drops: 2/3 chance of experience dropping

Best Tool to Use: Pickaxe

The most plentiful ore is Coal, and that's good because you're going to need a whole lot of it. Coal is what makes Torches, which are the primary light source in your game. Without Coal, you won't have any Torches, and you probably won't be able to see. Luckily, you can either burn Wood in Furnaces to make Charcoal or find Coal deposits easily in formations. Both work the same, despite their different names. Coal is also one of the best fuels for smelting in Furnaces (behind Lava Buckets and Blaze Rods). Covet your Coal, kids.

IRON

Found: Overworld from layer 1-63

Used In: Iron tools and armor, Buckets, Minecarts, Cauldron, Rails, Flint and Steel, Compass, Piston, Iron Door, and Iron Bars

Best Tool to Use: Stone Pickaxe or better required

If Diamond is the most coveted ore, Iron is the second, because Iron is necessary for so many important items. Whether building a railway with Minecarts, moving Water orLlava, setting a Nether Portal alight, trying to make a Map or even just mine Diamond and other rare materials, you'll need Iron. Iron is pretty common, luckily, though not nearly so as Coal. Look for it underground below sea level.

GOLD

Found: Overworld from layer 1-32

Used In: Gold Ingot, which makes Gold tools and Armor, Golden Apples, Clocks and Powered Rails

Best Tool to Use: Iron Pickaxe or better required

Gold is a very rare ore, with only 0.1473% of the underground of the world having Gold Ore in it. It can be crafted into Gold Ingots, whose main use is to craft Clocks, Golden Apples and Powered Rails. Gold items like tools and armor are weak, but can be enchanted, though the benefits rarely outweigh the cost. Gold tools are however the fastest mining tools in the game, but they also break the easiest (even easier than Wood tools).

DIAMOND

Found: Overworld from layer 1-16

Used In: Diamond tools and armor, Jukebox, Enchantment Table

Best Tool to Use: Iron Pickaxe or better required

Diamond is king. No seriously, in Minecraft, you want Diamond, more Diamond and all the Diamond. This is because Diamond makes the second fastest and longest lasting tools in the game at mining and harvesting, it can mine any other block, it makes the best weapons and armor and it's necessary for some recipes. Unfortunately, Diamond is also the hardest material to find, behind Emerald. Diamond is only in small deposits in the bottom 16 layers of the game, and it's only mineable with an Iron or Diamond Pickaxe. To find Diamond, you'll need to look in those low levels and try to find Lava, which it's often nearby. A note: you need Diamond tools to mine Obsidian, which you need to get to the Nether, which you probably need to do to get to The End.

NETHER QUARTZ ORE

Found: The Nether

Used In: Drops Nether Quartz Crystal, used in Comparators and Daylight Sensors (not yet in console) and Nether Quartz Blocks

Best Tool to Use: Wooden Pickaxe or better required

There's only one ore found in the Nether, and that's Nether Quartz. This is about as common as Iron and found on all layers of the Nether, but as of right now, the items that its drop (Nether Quartz Crystal) is used for are not yet implemented in the console version of the game. This should change soon.

REDSTONE

Found: Overworld from layer 1-16

Used In: Redstone mechanisms and circuits, Compass, Clock, Note Block

Best Tool to Use: Iron Pickaxe or better required

Another mineral found deep, deep down, Redstone is much more common than Diamond, and in fact will drop multiple pieces of Redstone for each block. It's one of the most interesting materials in the game due to it being the thing you need to create powered circuits and mechanisms. Redstone placed by itself acts like a wire connecting mechanisms to each other and power (which comes from Redstone Torches, Buttons, Levers or Pressure Plates), and when used with those mechanisms and other Redstone items, you can create complex machinery and devices. Look for Redstone by Lava.

LAPIS LAZULI

Found: Overworld from layer 1-32

Used In: dying things blue

Best Tool to Use: Stone Pickaxe or better required

Lapis Lazuli is fairly rare in the game, but it also drops multiple pieces when it breaks, and it's not used for anything except to dye Wool blue. It's fun to come across, especially if you love blue, but it isn't as valuable as some of the other ores.

EMERALD ORE

Found: Overworld only in Extreme Hills Biomes between layers 4-32

Used In: Drops Emeralds, used to trade with Villagers

Best Tool to Use: Iron Pickaxe or better required

By far the rarest mineral in Minecraft, the Emerald Ore block is only found in the Extreme Hills Biome and there are usually somewhere between 3-8 blocks of it per chunk in such Biomes. When mined, it drops 1 Emerald, which is used to trade with Villagers to procure items. Emeralds are highly prized by players, as the items that can be procured with them tend to be very valuable.

"NATURAL" MATERIALS

These are materials you'll come across in the world that aren't used in building except indirectly. In fact, you can only even pick up Water or Lava, but all of these natural materials have particular features that are worth noting.

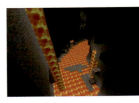

LAVA

Found: Overworld, the Nether
Uses: Defenses, decorations, building trash cans, creating Obsidian

Lava is found in pools on the surface of the Overworld, in underground caves and, most commonly, all over the Nether. It damages almost all creatures that touch it, and it also lights them on fire. This makes it dangerous, but also useful as a defensive decoration. You need Lava to make Obsidian, which happens when running Water hits still Lava. Its biggest use, however, is perhaps its ability to destroy unwanted blocks. You can then set up a pit of Lava in your shelter to throw unwanted items into, where they will be destroyed.

Note: Bookshelves, Leaves, Wool, Fences (but not gates), Vines, TNT, tall grass, Wood Planks, and Wooden Stairs are flammable and will be lit on fire by Lava.

SNOW

Found: Cold Biomes in the Overworld
Drops: Snowballs

Snow is mostly a decoration that sits on top of blocks, but if broken, it drops Snowballs. These can be used to create Snow Blocks, which can then be used as decoration or to make Snow Golems.

GRASS

Found: the Overworld
Drops: Grass Seeds

Similar to snow, grass doesn't do much, but it does break into Seeds. Seeds are used to grow Wheat, and are thus worth keeping in your stockpile.

MYCELIUM

Found: in the Mushroom Biome in the Overworld
Uses: Growing Mushrooms

Mycelium is another growing material that sits on top of blocks in the Mushroom Biome. It doesn't drop anything and can't be picked up, but it can be used to grow Mushrooms, which grow faster on mycelium.

Water

Found: the Overworld in any area
Uses: farming, creating Obsidian, putting out fire, decoration, shelter defenses, damaging Endermen

Water is important in Minecraft. You need it to farm, first of all, but you also want to have some with you most of the time when exploring so that you can put yourself out if you light on fire. Water is also used in decorating, in building barriers or traps for hostile mobs and in creating Obsidian, which occurs when running Water touches still Lava. Endermen are also damaged by Water easily, and it has a high blast resistance, making it a good tool for attacking and defending. Water can be carried in Buckets.

CRAFTABLE MATERIALS

Other than for building, materials are gathered in Minecraft in order to turn them into other items with your Crafting Table. Of these there are many, and since half of the fun is discovering what materials create what kind of items, we're just going to give a basic breakdown of the types of things you can craft in the game.

TOOLS

Of course, the most important thing to craft is tools. Without tools, you're going to have a very slow and incomplete experience, so they're very important to know about.

Tools in the game come in five varieties: Wooden, Stone, Iron, Gold and Diamond. Leaving out Gold tools, which break easily (though they mine quickest), the other tools are tough, mine quickly and can mine the most types of materials in this order Wooden<Stone<Iron<Diamond. In fact, you need a tool of the material before each in that order to even mine the next one.

Tools come in many varieties: Shovel, Hoe, Axe, Pickaxe, Shears and Fishing Pole. Some people consider Maps, Compasses, Buckets etc. to be tools, but we think it's simplest to stick with the definition that tools are items that are used to mine or harvest materials.

WEAPONS AND ARMOR

Like tools, armor as well as one weapon (the sword) are made of different materials, each of which is better than the last. The order of strength goes Leather<Gold<Iron<Diamond. There is also Chain armor in the game, which is between Gold and Iron in strength, but there is no natural way to get this in Survival at the moment. The other weapon in the game is the Bow, which is a ranged weapon made from a Stick and String.

MATERIAL REFINING

Crafting Table: Your basic item-creation station

Furnace: Refines ores, makes Charcoal and cooks food

Enchantment Table: Enchants items with power-ups

Brewing Stand: Creates potions with buffs and debuffs as well as attacks

Cauldrons: Hold Water, used to be for brewing before Brewing Stand was added

Anvil: Repair items, can also be dropped to cause damage below them

MECHANISMS

Everything you use for Redstone devices! This includes Buttons, Levers, Pistons and more, and they're some of the more complex and difficult-to-master items in the game. Play around with a few and a bit of Redstone, and you can create anything from a food dispenser to a trapdoor to even a working computer.

TRANSPORTATION

Rails, Minecarts and Boats fall in this category. This is everything you can create that helps you move without using your feet.

FOOD

Though not all food is crafted, some is, and others are cooked in the Furnace to make them better. Food is necessary in survival mode, and it comes in a wide variety of types. Food items are either used as ingredients in food that can be eaten, or they can be cooked or eaten themselves.

All Other Items

You'd think with a list this big that we'd be done, but nope! There are dozens of other items out there in the world of Minecraft, many of which are rare and difficult to acquire. We've covered everything we think is essential above, so we'll leave it to you to discover the other unique items in the game for yourself! Good luck, and here's a hint: keep on exploring. You never know what you'll find in the next chest.

DECORATIONS

Some folks are all about the building, some love adventure, and some love to design cool houses. Minecraft obliges this last group of Minecrafters by providing ample items to spruce up that shelter, including colored Wool blocks, Paintings and much more.

FRIENDS & FOES

It only takes a few seconds in Survival Mode to realize that your character in Minecraft is not alone. Nope, the world of Minecraft is a full one, teeming with everything from tiny Chickens to Wolves to Zombie Pigmen to the giant Ghast, and if you're going to thrive in this crowded land, you're gonna need to know a bit about these creatures, known as "mobs."

Notes:

1. This section focuses on location, behavior, drops and combat. For breeding, see the Mining & Farming section.

2. The Attack stats are approximate. Attack can change somewhat depending on circumstances and exact numbers have yet to be confirmed for the Xbox 360 console version of the game.

3. Health, Armor and Attack are measured in half-icons, so 1 "heart" icon = 2 Health, one "sword" icon = 2 Attack, and one "chestplate" icon = 2 Armor.

PEACEFUL MOBS

There are quite a few mobs out there that won't ever attack you, no matter how many times you punch them in the face or otherwise pester them. These mobs are considered "peaceful."

SHEEP

Sheep are everywhere, they are not smart and you will need them for Beds. Sheep tend to spawn in flocks and then roam about, and since they can both jump 1 block high and swim, they end up all over the place.

Sheep are usually white (81.836% chance) but can also spawn as dark grey, light grey, or black (5%), brown (3%) or pink (0.164%), and whatever color they are is the color of Wool you will get from them. Wool can be gathered either by killing the Sheep or by using Shears on it (1 block for killing, 1-3 for shearing). You can also dye sheep to change the color of their Wool.

IRON GOLEM

The mighty Iron Golem! These tough dudes spawn naturally in Villages with 10 Villagers and 21 houses or more, and they serve to protect the Village from Zombie sieges. Additionally, players can craft them with 4 Blocks of Iron in a T formation with a Pumpkin stuck on top as the head. They are very powerful, but they will only protect Villagers, not the player, and they will wander away from the player if there is nothing keeping them from doing so (a barrier).

MOOSHROOM

A rarer version of the Cow, the Mooshroom is a Cow that's been infected by Mushrooms. You can only find these guys in the uncommon Mushroom Biome, but they're even better than Cows for food and materials.

This is because, in addition to what a Cow drops, you can also get infinite Mushroom Stew (3 food units, 7.2 hunger saturation). On top of that, if you ever really need Mushrooms, you can use Shears on the Mooshroom and get 5.

CHICKEN

Chickens may be small and easy to kill, but they also drop a ton of useful items and are easy to farm. You usually find Chickens spread out across the ground and Water,

and they can fall without taking damage, so they can end up in deep pits and ravines.

Chickens drop three potential food items: Eggs (used in cooking), Raw Chicken (2 units of the food bar, 1.2 hunger saturation [see Farming & Mining for more info], 30% chance of food poisoning) or Cooked Chicken (3 food units, 7.2 hunger saturation) if it was killed by fire. Chickens also drop Feathers, which are used in crafting Arrows.

COW

Another pack wanderer, Cows often spawn in groups of 4-10 then wander off, sometimes even falling down cliffs and killing themselves.

Cows are one of the best sources of food, as Raw Beef gives 3 food units and 1.8 hunger saturation (no risk of poison), Steak gives 4 food units and 12.8 hunger saturation and Milk is used to cure status effects like poison and in cooking Cakes. Steak is the most balanced food item in the game, and Milk is infinite, making Cows

very good to farm. Their other drop, Leather, is used in crafting the lowest level of armor.

OCELOT/CAT

Released when the Jungle Biome was added to the various versions of the game, the Ocelot/Cat is the cat lover's answer to the Wolf/Dog, and it's both super cute and super useful. Though they do not attack or cause damage at all, when tamed with an uncooked Fish, the Ocelot turns into a Cat. The Cat can either follow the character or be told to sit, and it will scare Creepers away from whatever area it's in! This makes Cats insanely useful at a base or important parts of your map. To tame, simply hold out an un-cooked Fish and wait 'til an Ocelot approaches. Feed the Fish to the Ocelot, and there's a 1/3 chance it'll turn into a Cat. Both Cats and Ocelots can breed by putting them into love mode with Fish.

PIG

Pigs spawn just about everywhere that's not underground, and their initial group is 3-4 Pigs, so you can often find quite a few together.

Pig meat comes as Raw or Cooked Porkchops, and it gives identical health benefits to Raw Beef and Steak, respectively (3 food units, 1.8 hunger saturation / 4 food units, 12.8 hunger saturation), making Pigs a good source of food.

It is possible to find a Saddle in a Chest, put it on the Pig and ride it around. To control the movement of the Pig, you need a Carrot on a Stick equipped.

WOLF

Though they start out neutral and will become hostile if attacked (and will attack in groups), Wolves can be "tamed" by feeding them Bones. You'll know a Wolf is successfully tamed when it gets a collar around its neck and starts following you.

Tamed wolves follow the player and attack any mobs that attack the player or are attacked by the player except Creepers. They are most effective versus Zombies and Skeletons, less against Spiders, Cave Spiders and Endermen and almost not at all against Creepers, Magma Cubes and Slimes.

You can tell the health of a Wolf by the angle that its tail is pointing. A tail that is all the way up means full health, and all the way down means very low health, with corresponding positions in-between. To raise the health of your Wolf, feed it any meat, including Rotten Flesh (which won't hurt it).

Wolves also have special behavioral traits when it comes to mobility. A Wolf told to follow you that gets outside of a 20x20x10 block from the player will automatically teleport to the player, unless there's no room for it to do so. Additionally, you can tell a wolf to "sit" with Left Trigger, which makes it stay where it is until otherwise ordered.

SQUID

The only Water mob out there, the Squid will not attack and just drops Ink Sacs. They do make cool pets if you can trap them, though.

SNOW GOLEM

Snow Golems are creatures that are crafted by stacking two Snow Blocks on top of each other (4 Snowballs = 1 Snow Block) and topping it off with a Pumpkin.

Snow Golems are very weak and do no damage to any creature except Blazes and the Ender Dragon, and they are damaged by the Nether, Deserts, Jungles and Water of any kind. However, they do throw Snowballs at most hostile mobs (not Creepers, however), which pushes the mob back slightly and keeps them away when used in groups.

VILLAGER

Villagers hang out in, not surprisingly, Villages, and they can breed with each other and trade with the player. Each Villager has a profession (Farmer, Librarian, Priest, Blacksmith, Butcher), and you can trade with them for profession-related items. Typically, Villagers request Emeralds for the items they offer for trade.

ZOMBIE PIGMAN

All over the Nether, you'll find Zombie Pigmen, usually in groups. They spawn in fours, but can gather together in larger groups, and they hang out in most parts of the Nether.

Like Villagers, this mob is humanoid and initially neutral to the player, but unlike Villagers, Zombie Pigmen most definitely will attack you if you hurt one. In fact, attacking a Pigman alerts any other Pigmen within a 32 block radius, who will all go hostile and come at the player with Swords.

HOSTILE MOBS

Now, these are the guys in Minecraft who want nothing more than to bite you, poison you, shoot you full of arrows, light you on fire, punch you in the face, blow you up and otherwise attempt to make you no more. Even with the best gear, a few of these guys ganging up on you can mean a quick death, often far from home, especially if you don't know their tendencies and weaknesses. Get familiar with these guys as much as possible, and it most definitely will save your life.

CREEPER

Ah, the Creeper. He's the unofficial mascot of the game, the sneakiest mob and the one you'll find yourself most dreading.

When Creepers get within two blocks of you (so one separating), their "countdown" starts, and you have 1.5 seconds before it blows up all of the blocks in about a 6x6x6 area around it. Yep, it's a pain. The only warning you get for this is a slight "hiss" sound when it gets close, and since they will attack any players they see within 16 blocks and are good at finding paths to you, it's pretty likely that you'll have at least one Creeper death in your Minecraft experience. This is made even more likely by the fact that they can survive in daylight, unlike most hostile mobs.

The good news is that Creepers can't blow up when they see you through Glass or a Door, and if you kill them from a distance or before they can do their countdown, they will die without exploding and will even drop Gunpowder, which you can use to make TNT. A harder drop to get from a Creeper is a Music Disc, which requires the Creeper be killed by a Skeleton's Arrow.

Because of their ability to blow up your hard work, it's best to protect yourself from Creepers by paying attention to your surroundings and building safely where they can't get to you. Because, as they say, that'sssssss a very nice house you've got there...It'd be a sssssshame if anything were to happen to it.

SPIDER

You're gonna see a lot of Spiders. Spiders are neutral until they've been exposed to darkness or attacked. This means that a Spider found in daylight will be neutral, but if he happens to wander into a dark area, he's gonna go hostile and stay that way. Spiders that start off in dark areas and move to light will remain hostile, however.

Despite their small attack, Spiders are dangerous because they can climb walls as if all blocks had Ladders on them and they can jump up to 3 blocks high. They also can see players through walls, meaning that if there's a hostile Spider within 16 blocks of you, it knows you're there and is trying to get to you, and they can even fit through one block high spaces.

To be safe around Spiders, wear armor, carry weapons and make sure your shelter is enclosed and well-lit. If you do kill a Spider, it may drop the very useful String or Spider Eyes.

SPIDER JOCKEY

A very rare mob, these have a 1% chance of spawning anytime a Spider does. They include a Skeleton archer riding on top of a Spider, both of which otherwise behave normally and take damage individually. Because of this, Spider Jockeys spawn, move and see like Spiders, though the Skeleton will simply attack anytime it sees you, whether the Spider is hostile or not. On top of that, the Skeleton can suffocate or burn in daylight, leaving the Spider on its own.

SKELETON

Skeletons are major pests in Minecraft because they spawn just about everywhere there's darkness and they attack with arrows from a distance. If you're being attacked in a dark cave and you can't see where it's coming from, then you've probably found a Skeleton.

Skeleton attacks don't do huge damage, however, and can even be entirely prevented by armor. You will want to make sure your shelter is completely sealed, however, because they can shoot through gaps. Skeletons also burn up in daylight.

Skeletons have two very useful drops when killed: Bones and Arrows. Bones can be turned into Bonemeal for use in farming, and picking up Arrows from Skeletons is a lot easier than crafting them.

ZOMBIE

Another of the most common mobs, Zombies wander around the Overworld at night looking for you and your fleshy friends so they can feed on you. Zombies also attack Villages in swarms called Zombie Sieges and can eventually break down doors, both in Villages and otherwise.

Zombies attack by touching you, and they can quickly take your health down if they trap you in a small area. The main reason for killing Zombies, other than survival, is that they drop Rotten Flesh. This stuff can be eaten by your character in an emergency (4 food units, 80% chance of poisoning), but its main use is to feed tame Wolves. Like many mobs, Zombies burn during daylight.

ENDERMAN

From the deep, dark lands of The End, the Endermen come to the Overworld to shift blocks around, look awesome and punch you for looking at them. No joke. Endermen are special mobs that aren't hostile to start, but if you're within 64 blocks and your crosshair points at an Enderman above their legs, they will come at you.

Endermen have a pretty tough attack, which is made worse by their ability to teleport around. This also means they can show up almost anywhere, though they tend to avoid sunlight, rain and Water. Sunlight, rain, Water and fire make them neutral, and any contact with Water damages an Enderman—useful tips for combat. It's suggested to attack the legs as well, as the Enderman can't teleport when taking leg damage.

Fighting an Enderman can be necessary when attempting to go to The End, because finding the necessary Ender Pearls otherwise can be very difficult.

CAVE SPIDER

You won't run into Cave Spiders very often, as they only spawn in Abandoned Mineshafts from Monster Spawners, but they're much tougher than regular Spiders. To deal with Cave Spiders, you'll have to fight your way to their spawner and either break it or disable it.

Doing that is more than likely going to mean a bite or two from a Cave Spider, and since they're poisonous, you'll want to bring some Milk to counteract the effects.

SILVERFISH

Silverfish hang out in fake blocks called Monster Eggs in Strongholds and in caves in the Extreme Hills Biome. The Silverfish can make a Monster Egg out of a Cobblestone, Stone or Stone Brick block, and you can tell it's a Monster Egg by it taking longer than normal to break with a tool or quicker without one.

Breaking a Monster Egg releases a hostile Silverfish, and if it is attacked and not killed, it will wake every Silverfish in a 21x11x21 block radius and make them attack as well. Silverfish do damage every time you make a change on the Y axis (vertical) in relation to the Silverfish. You also hop every time you're damaged, which is a change on the Y axis, so Silverfish can do damage quickly.

SLIME

Only spawning below level 40, Slimes have three sizes. When the Slime is killed, it splits into 2-4 more Slimes of the next smallest size until it is made tiny and killed again.

Slimes are great for experience and are further useful for their drop, Slimeballs, which are used to make Sticky Pistons and Magma Cream. They are also one of the few hostile mobs that can survive sunlight.

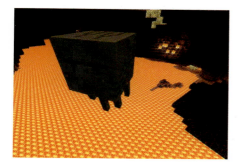

GHAST

The scourges of the Nether, Ghasts are huge and shoot at you with explosive fireballs from up to 100 blocks away. These fireballs do 17 damage at close range (8.5 hearts), but they also light the area around on fire, which deals more damage.

To defeat Ghasts, you'll need to build shelters that protect you from their line of site, and hit the Ghast fireballs away with your hand or item. Ghasts drop Gunpowder like Creepers as well as Ghast Tears, a potion ingredient.

Magma Cube

Similar to Slimes, Magma Cubes are hopping creatures found in the Nether that also split into smaller Magma Cubes. The main differences, besides their appearance, is that they can survive falls, Lava and Water, jump 4 blocks high and do more damage than a Slime.

As with Slime, Magma Cubes are great for experience, and they also drop Magma Cream, another potion ingredient.

Blaze

If you're looking for Blaze Powder, you'll need to find a Blaze, and these tough mobs only show up in Nether Forts. There, Blazes will start popping out once you're within 16 blocks of a Blaze Spawner and can spawn 1-4 at a time, meaning they will build in numbers quickly.

The best method for defeating Blazes is to kill those spawned by using weapons and Snowballs (which do 3 damage to the Blaze). While doing so, destroy or disable the Monster Spawner to avoid more. Snow Golems are also good against Blazes, but will melt in the Nether.

Blazes carry two rare items: Blaze Rods (used in creating Brewing Stands and Blaze Powder) and Glowstone Dust (used in brewing and making Glowstone). Since Blaze Powder is necessary to make an Eye of Ender (among other things), which you need to get to The End, many players find themselves needing to hunt Blazes at some point.

Ender Dragon

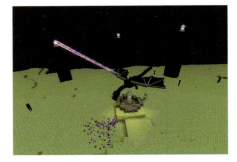

There's no greater foe in Minecraft than the Ender Dragon, and there are few greater challenges. Located in The End, the Ender Dragon has 200 health points and does huge damage in the Xbox 360 console version (the PC version has different attacks).

The Ender Dragon also gains health by having it beamed from a circle of Obsidian pillars that have Ender Crystals on the top. These will need to be destroyed before you can kill the Ender Dragon, either by shooting them with Arrows or (in the case of the caged Crystals) building to them and breaking them.

It's recommended to take enchanted Diamond weapons and armor and a lot of Obsidian to build with (it won't blow up like most blocks) to defeat the mighty Ender Dragon. Once you do, you'll be rewarded with 12,000 experience (enough to get you to level 78) and the infamous End Poem.

PEACEFUL MOBS

Friend/Foe	Found	Health	Exp.	Drop	Follows (when in hand)
SHEEP	Overworld	8 (4 Hearts)	1-3	Wool (1, 1-3 if dropped)	Wheat
CHICKEN	Overworld	4 (2 Hearts)	1-3	Feathers (0-2) Raw Chicken (1) Cooked Chicken (1 if killed by fire) Egg (1 every 5-10 minutes if alive)	Any seed
COW	Overworld	10 (5 Hearts)	1-3	Leather (0-2) Raw Beef (1-3) Steak (1-3 if killed by fire) Milk (when Bucket is used on it)	Wheat
MOOSHROOM	Overworld (Mushroom Biome)	10 (5 Hearts)	1-3	Leather (0-2) Raw Beef (1-3) Steak (1-3 if killed by fire) Milk (when Bucket is used on it) Mushroom Stew (when Bowl is used on it) Red Mushroom (5 when sheared)	Wheat
PIG	Overworld	10 (5 Hearts)	1-3	Raw Porkchop (1-3) Cooked Porkchop (1-3 if killed by fire)	Wheat

Friend/Foe	Found	Health	Attack	Exp.	Drop	Follows (when in hand)
WOLF	Overworld (spawns on grass)	Wild: 8 (4 Hearts) Tamed: 20 (10)	Wild: 2 (1 Heart) Tamed: 4	1-3	None	Bone

Friend/Foe	Found	Health	Exp.	Drop
SQUID	Overworld (Water, spawns between levels 46-62)	10 (5 Hearts)	1-3	Ink Sac (1-3)
VILLAGER	Overworld (Villages)	20 (10 Hearts)	0	Nothing

Friend/Foe	Found	Health	Armor	Attack	Exp.	Drop
ZOMBIE PIGMAN	The Nether, rarely in the Overworld	20 (10 Hearts)	2	Easy: 5 Normal: 9 Hard: 13	5	Rotten Flesh (0-1)

Friend/Foe	Found	Health	Attack	Exp.	Drop
SNOW GOLEM	Created	4 (2 Hearts)	0 (only pushes most mobs) 3 (Blazes only) 1 (Ender Dragon)	0	Snowball (0-15)
OVERWORLD	Jungle	10 (5 hearts)	None (scares Creepers, however)	1-3	None
OVERWORLD/ NETHER	Villages or Crafted by Player	100 (50 hearts)	7-21 (3.5-10.5 hearts)	0	Iron Ingot (3-5) Poppy (0-2)

HOSTILE MOBS

Friend/Foe	Found	Spawns	Health	Attack	Exp.	Drop
CREEPER	Overworld or Nether	Light Level: 7 or less	20 (10 Hearts)	Depends on how close, Maximum: 49 (24.5 hearts)	5	Gunpowder (0-2 when killed but not exploded) Music Disc (when killed by an arrow from a Skeleton)
SPIDER	Overworld	Light Level: 7 or Less, But Can Survive in Light (goes Peaceful)	16 (8 Hearts)	Easy: 2 Normal: 2 Hard: 3	5	String (0-2) Spider Eye (0-1
SPIDER JOCKEY	Overworld	Light Level: 7 or Less, But Can Survive in Light (goes Peaceful)	Spider: 16 (8 Hearts) Skeleton: 20 (10)	Spider- Easy: 2 Normal: 2 Hard: 3 Skeleton- Easy: 2	5 for each	Spider: String (0-2) Spider Eye (0-1) Skeleton: Bone (0-2) Arrow (0-2)
SKELETON	Overworld or Nether	Light Level: 7 or less	20 (10 Hearts)	Easy: 2 Normal:3-4 Hard: 4-6	5	Arrow (0-2) Bone (0-2)

Friend/Foe	Found	Spawns	Armor	Health	Attack	Exp.	Drop
ZOMBIE	Overworld or Nether	Light Level: 7 or Less	2	20 (10 Hearts)	3-6 depending on health	5	Rotten Flesh Rare: Carrot, Iron Ingot, Potato

Friend/Foe	Found	Spawns	Health	Attack	Exp.	Drop
ENDERMAN	Overworld or The End	Light Level: 7 or Less	40 (20 Hearts)	Easy: 4 Normal: 7 Hard: 10	5	Ender Pearl (0-1)
CAVE SPIDER	Overworld (Abandoned Mineshafts)	From Monster Spawner in Mineshaft Only	12 (6 Hearts)	Easy: 2 Normal: 2 (Poisoned) Hard: 3 (Poisoned) Poison Damage: 1 Every 1.5 seconds Normal: 7 Seconds Hard: 15 Seconds	5	String (0-2) Spider Eye (0-1)

HOSTILE MOBS

Friend/Foe	Found	Spawns	Health	Attack	Exp.	Drop
SILVERFISH	Overworld (Strongholds and Rarely Underground in Extreme Hills Biomes)	From Monster Spawner (Strongholds) or Monster Egg (Fake Blocks, Strongholds and Extreme Hills Biomes)	8 (4 Hearts)	1	5	None
SLIME	Overworld	Below Level 40	Big: 16 (8 Hearts) Small: 4 (2) Tiny: 1 (0)	Big: 4 Small: 2 Tiny: 0	Big: 4 Small: 2 Tiny: 1	Slimeball (0-2, only from Tiny Slime)
GHAST	The Nether	Anywhere with space except in Nether Fortresses	10 (5 Hearts)	More the closer it gets, Max of 17	5	Gunpowder (0-2) Ghast Tear (0-1)

Friend/Foe	Found	Spawns	Armor	Health	Attack	Exp.	Drop
MAGMA CUBE	The Nether	Anywhere, often near Nether Fortresses	Big: 12 Small: 6 Tiny: 3	Big: 16 (8 Hearts) Small: 4 (2) Tiny: 1 (1/2)	Big: 6 Small: 4 Tiny: 3	5	Magma Cream (0-1, only Big and Small)

Friend/Foe	Found	Spawns	Health	Attack	Exp.	Drop
BLAZE	The Nether (Nether Fortresses)	Light Level 11 or Less or Monster Spawners, both in Nether Fortresses	20 (10 Hearts)	Fireball- Easy: 3 Normal: 5 Hard: 7 Contact- Easy: 4 Normal: 6 Hard: 9	10	Blaze Rod (0-1) Glowstone (0-2)
ENDER DRAGON	The End	In The End	200 (100 Hearts)	Fireball: Unknown, similar to Ghast Acid Spray: Unknown, very strong	12,000	Nothing

Villages often have farms.

NAVIGATION

If there's one thing that Minecraft is all about besides building, it's exploring, and this game does not slouch when it comes to giving you cool things to find. In fact, even a player that's plugged hundreds of hours into Minecraft can climb just one more mountain or break into just one more cavern and come across a gorgeous view that they've never seen in the game.

The world you see in Minecraft is essentially broken down into natural environments (Biomes) and environments spawned from building materials (Structures). In the Xbox 360 console version of Minecraft, there are currently four major Structures and two minor Structures, each of which has its own rules for where it can occur, what type of creatures populate it and what can be found or done within it. Knowing this info can make a big difference in your gameplay, especially when attempting to survive at the beginning of a game or when looking for certain items later on. There's nothing like coming across a Chest of Diamond right when you need it!

Note: when exploring just about any of these, except the Village, you'll want to bring plenty of Torches or other items to mark your path, or you most definitely will get lost.

Village by night.

Villages are great places to find resources.

Item	Quantity	Weight	Chance
Bread	1 - 3	15	62%
Apple	1 - 3	15	62%
Iron Ingot	1 - 5	10	47%
Iron Sword	1	5	27%
Iron Pickaxe	1	5	27%
Iron Helmet	1	5	27%
Iron Chestplate	1	5	27%
Iron Leggings	1	5	27%
Iron Boots	1	5	27%
Oak Sapling	3 - 7	5	27%
Obsidian	3 - 11	5	27%
Gold Ingot	1 - 3	5	27%
Diamond	1 - 3	3	17%

VILLAGES

If you're running around the Overworld (the part of the game spawn in), and you see a cluster of houses and think "Hey, I didn't build that!", you probably just found a Village. Villages are collections of buildings populated by neutral Villagers.

WHERE

Villages only spawn in Plains or Desert Biomes. They tend to spawn where it's flat, but they can also spawn on hills and across ravines, which can make for strange set-ups.

STRUCTURES

Depending on the available space, the game will place certain structures in a Village. The Hut, Butcher's Shop, Small House and Large House are simple structures made of Wood, Wood Planks and Cobble, and they usually contain a Villager or two. The Watch Tower and Church are taller structures with great views and a Villager, and you can also find Wells and Lamp Posts (made of one Black Wool block and some Torches). The most important Village structures, however, are the Farms, Library and Blacksmith, which contain useful items and in which Villagers live that can be traded with.

MOBS

The only mobs native to Villages are Villagers, baby Villagers and Iron Golems. Adult Villagers have professions and will breed with each other, and you can trade Emeralds with Villagers for various resources. You may also see Zombies attacking Villages in Zombie Sieges.

MATERIALS

Villages are excellent places to raid for building materials in a pinch, as they're made of things like Wood Planks and Cobblestone. The best resources, however, are found at the Farms, the Library and the Blacksmith. Farms yield Wheat and Wheat Seeds, which means you can easily make Bread or start your own Wheat Farm. Libraries contain Books (helpful for Enchanting) and a Crafting Table you can snatch up. The Blacksmith, however, has a couple Furnaces and the true treasure: a Chest of items. Check out the graph to the left to see what goodies you can expect in a Blacksmith's Chest.

A Stronghold library.

Beware of mobs in Strongholds.

STRONGHOLDS

At some point in the game, you'll either accidentally pop into one of these (often massive) structures, or you'll need to find one to get to The End. Strongholds can sometimes be small, but usually they're huge, confusing and highly dangerous. There are only three Strongholds per world.

WHERE

Find a Stronghold by throwing an Eye of Ender. The direction it flies toward is the direction of a Stronghold. If you don't have an Eye of Ender, you're going to have to just dig around until you crack into one. Strongholds are always at least 640 blocks from your start point and no farther than 1152, and they also often intersect sections like Ravines, Mineshafts and Caves.

STRUCTURES

Strongholds are mostly mazes of hallways, stairs and rooms, but they also include a few specific structures of note. These include Store Rooms, Libraries and the End Portal Room. Store Rooms are exactly what they sound like: an area that contains a Chest of useful stuff. Libraries are rooms full of Bookshelves and Cobwebs, and they come in one-story and two-story sizes. They also contain chests at the end of one or two bookshelves, depending on the size of the Library. The End Portal room is the only place in the world the player can get to The End, which is done by placing Eyes of Ender into the blocks of the End Portal, a structure that sits above a pool of Lava and is guarded by a Silverfish Monster Spawner.

MOBS

Fair warning: Strongholds are dangerous. They can contain just about every hostile mob in the Overworld, including Zombies, Skeletons, Spiders, Creepers and Silverfish. Silverfish are especially dangerous, as they can live in blocks called Monster Eggs that are disguised as normal blocks, and they attack in groups when one is damaged near others.

MATERIALS

Large parts of Strongholds are built out of materials that are hard to come by elsewhere, such as Iron Bars, Iron Doors, Buttons, and special Stone blocks like Mossy or Cracked Stone. Even better, the Chests in Strongholds carry some great items, with possibilities including Ender Pearls, Apples, Bread, Coal, Redstone, Armor, Iron Ingots, Iron Swords, Iron Pickaxes and, rarely, Diamond, Golden Apples or Saddles.

If you find an Abandoned Mineshaft, be ready for Cave Spiders.

Lucky players may find an Abandoned Mineshaft early and strip it of its Wood and other resources.

Item	Quantity per stack	Chance
Bread	1 - 3	20% (1/5)
Pumpkin Seeds	2 - 4	13% (2/15)
Melon Seeds	2 - 4	13% (2/15)
Iron Ingot	1 - 5	13% (2/15)
Coal	3 - 8	13% (2/15)
Redstone	4 - 9	7% (1/15)
Gold Ingot	1 - 3	7% (1/15)
Lapis Lazuli	4 - 9	7% (1/15)
Diamond	1 - 2	4% (1/25)
Rails	4 - 8	1.3% (1/75)
Iron Pickaxe	1	1.3% (1/75)
Enchanted Book	1	??% (??/??)

ABANDONED MINESHAFT

These are just what they sound like: mineshafts that spawn as if someone else had built them and then abandoned them.

WHERE

Randomly placed underground, especially intersecting with ravines and caves.

STRUCTURES

Mineshafts are simply hallways, stairways, crossings and rooms, often with Rail Tracks, supports and Minecarts in them.

MOBS

All mobs that can spawn in darkness have a chance of being in a Mineshaft, with the added danger of the smaller Cave Spider, which spawns from Monster Spawners and is unique to Abandoned Mineshafts. These little guys are poisonous, so watch out!

MATERIALS

If you plan on making anything out of Rails, breaking them up in Mineshafts is the most efficient method. Other simple materials such as Wood Planks, Fences and Torches can be found, as well as Chests, usually in Minecarts. See the chart at the left for likely Chest items.

Get ready to fight if you find a Dungeon.

Item stack	Chance of of spawning	Chance of finding a stack	Number in stack
Saddle	1/12	46.6%	1
Iron Ingot	1/12	46.6%	1-4
Bread	1/12	46.6%	1
Wheat	1/12	46.6%	1-4
Gunpowder	1/12	46.6%	1-4
String	1/12	46.6%	1-4
Bucket	1/12	46.6%	1
Enchanted Book	1/120	46.6%	1
Redstone	1/12	26.4%	1-4
13 disc	1/12	5.8%	1
cat disc	1/12	5.8%	1
Golden Apple (Normal)	1/120	0.6%	1

DUNGEON

Small rooms randomly placed about the map, Dungeons contain a Monster Spawner and a Chest or two of items.

WHERE

Just about anywhere, but often in caves. Look for Mossy Stone and Cobblestone: those two together usually indicate a Dungeon.

STRUCTURES

Nothing more than one simple room!

MOBS

There will probably be tons of mobs of whatever type of Monster Spawner is in there (Zombie, Skeleton or Spider). Beware!

MATERIALS

Just Cobble and Mossy Stone and the Monster Spawner, besides what's in the Chest.

TEMPLES

Temples are awesome structures that look like big pyramids and which contain traps and Chests that contain useful items.

WHERE

Temples are only found in Jungles or in Deserts, and the two versions look slightly different from each other.

STRUCTURES

Both types of Temples are comprised of just one big building. Inside Jungle Temples, you'll find a puzzle that consists of three Levers and some Sticky Pistons. Desert Temples, on the other hand, have a secret room under a block of blue Wool. In the room is a trap consisting of a Stone Pressure Plate wired up to a large amount of TNT that will go off if the Plate is pressed. Also in the room will be 4 Chests with random loot from the same list as the Jungle Temple, making Desert Temples highly sought-after.

Nether Fortresses are not to be lightly trifled with.

A Zombie Pigman stands guard over a crop of Nether Wart.

NETHER FORTRESSES

The only Structure found in the Nether, these are enormous, hugely dangerous and are the only place to find Nether Wart and Blazes. They're not too hard to find, but getting out alive requires great gear, patience and skill.

WHERE

The Nether, of course! Walk around long enough, and you're likely to find one, especially in big rooms, and when you do, the other Nether Forts will be laid out to the north and south in strips.

STRUCTURES

Nether Fortresses are comprised of tower-like structures connected by bridges. There are a few special rooms in the Forts: a stairwell with Nether Wart in it (the only place to find it), rooms with Blaze Spawners (also unique) and halls or rooms with Chests.

MOBS

You're most likely to come across Skeletons, Blazes and Magma Cubes in Nether Fortresses, while Ghasts may float above the bridges and Zombie Pigmen might be nearby. The rule for Nether Forts is to go in heavily armored and with the best weapons possible, as you will be attacked.

MATERIALS

Besides the Nether Brick they're made of, which is immune to Ghast fireballs, and the items that spawn in chests (Iron Ingots, Gold Ingots, Golden Chestplates and Swords, Saddles, Flint and Steel, Nether Wart and Diamonds are possible), Nether Forts are also the only place to get Blaze Rods (from killing Blazes) and Nether Wart, both of which are essential for crafting certain items (especially potions). You can also get Glowstone Dust from Blazes, occasionally.

GUIDE TO MINI-GAMES & ONLINE PLAY

Since even the earliest days of Minecraft, creative folks out there have been taking the rules of this blocky building game and have made entirely new games out of it! The many, many kinds of mini-games people have come up with inside of Minecraft is frankly amazing, and in fact some of them are so much fun that many players now do nothing but play them instead of the regular game!

This has especially become the norm for online Minecraft servers on the PC edition of the game, where mini-game playing has become an entire culture of its own. For those of you with the PC version, or those console or mobile players who are curious what kind of crazy things people have gotten up to with this game, here are 10 enormously popular Minecraft mini-games that change up the entire way you play the game, all in ways we love and think you will too.

PRISON

Like the name says, the idea here is that you are in prison, but here's the twist: it's fun! You begin as a prisoner in the lowest ranked "cell-block" (often Block D, but it can vary), and you work to earn money, which you then use to move up to higher ranked cell-blocks. Eventually, you can earn enough money to gain freedom, at which point you can either lord your wealth over the newbs or (on many servers) become a guard, and eventually even the warden of the prison.

In order to earn money you must collect resources within your cell-block to sell at special areas of the map. This is generally done by mining, cutting down trees for Wood, fishing and/or other regular resource collection activities. There will be specific areas in your cell-block to gather each resource, and these areas tend to reset every so often so that there are more delicious resources to acquire. You'll usually start off with some tools to allow you to get these needed resources, though on some Prison servers you will have to purchase replacements at a shop.

Here's where things get tricky: you can't just move around the whole prison as you like. While PvP isn't allowed within your cell-block or in designated safe zones, the areas between cell-blocks and sometimes even between the selling areas/shops/resource areas are free game as spaces for other prisoners to attack you and take your items. Additionally, you will need to make sure you are not performing any behavior that a guard could get you in trouble for, such as owning a weapon or hanging out in a cell-block above your rank.

As they say about real prison, keep your head down and do your work, and you'll survive. Of course, it can be a lot of fun to be the bad seed in the prison as well...

A Cops & Robbers prison isn't all about labor and hanging in your cell, but don't think that just because this basketball court is outside it's any easier to escape from.

COPS & ROBBERS

Similar but somewhat different to prison, Cops & Robbers also puts you in a prison as either a guard or a prisoner, but instead of having the goal of purchasing your freedom, you are attempting to escape the prison without the guard knowing and/or killing you.

As opposed to Prison's shared cell-blocks, in Cops & Robbers prisoners will usually have their very own individual cell. Each day, you will wake up and have to move around the prison on a schedule, performing tasks under the watch of the guards. If a guard asks you to do anything, you must comply immediately or risk punishment (such as losing items or being moved to a stronger cell) or even being killed.

There will be quite a few less guards than prisoners (maybe even just one guard), so the idea is that the guards can't watch everything all the time. Prisoners need to take advantage of any time they can sneak away or do something against the rules (like building weapons or digging escape tunnels) in order to work on escaping.

Winning is slightly different from server to server, but usually the prisoners win if they escape, and the guards win if no one or not enough prisoners have escaped after a certain amount of time.

A group of hiders rush to find good spots before the seeker is released.

HIDE 'N SEEK

A basic Hide 'n Seek game with one player trying to find a few others on a map is really easy to set up, and a lot of people play that way on their own maps. On servers, however, Hide 'n Seek is a little different.

The basic premise of hiding from a seeker is the same, but on servers that play Hide 'n Seek, the hiders have an extra advantage in that they appear to the seekers to look like regular blocks in the game! So, for instance, a hider might look like an Oak Wood block or a Fence post or a Glowstone lamp.

Each game starts with the hiders picking the type of block they want to be (some servers assign them randomly), and they are then given a minute or so to hide on a pre-made map. These maps are usually made so that there are a lot more of the type of block you choose to be, so you can go hide next to them. You want to make it look natural, so that the seeker will just run past, but don't worry about lining up perfectly with the other blocks- you will appear to be lined up and perfectly still as long as you put yourself squarely on a block and aren't walking, meaning you can look around all you like.

Seekers have a certain amount of time to find and kill all of the hiding blocks, and they are outfitted with armor and weapons. Hiders sometimes have a weak weapon, but they have to gang up on seekers to kill them generally. If the hiders make it through the time limit without dying, they win!

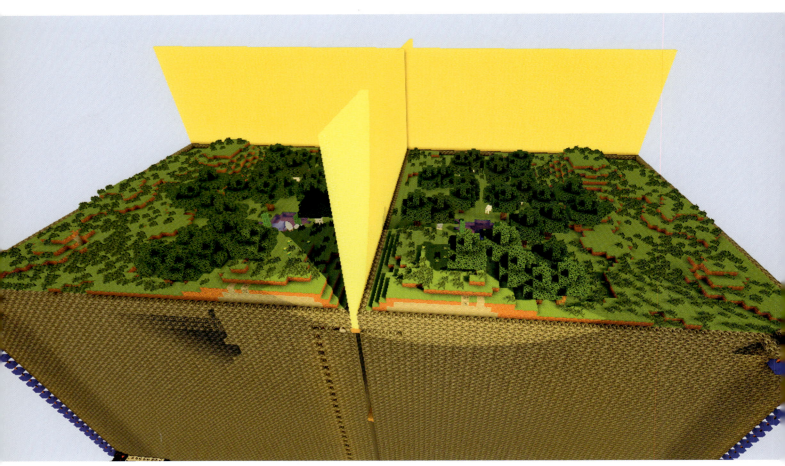

Above: The great and mighty Walls, before they're brought crashing down. Note the pit beneath the wall of Sand, where it disappears into. Bottom: A group of players on a server prepare to enter The Walls.

THE WALLS

One of the very most popular and commonly found mini-games, The Walls was made by the legendary Hypixel (check out their entry in our Heroes chapter), and it's essentially basic PvP with a twist.

You and 3 other players or teams are dropped into one quadrant of a regular Minecraft world that has limits (meaning it's only so big). There are giant sand walls dividing your quadrant of the map from the other players, and a huge timer floating above everything. You have the time until the timer reaches 0:00 to prepare your self and your area for battle, and once the timer does hit zero, the walls fall down!

At that point, it's an all-out brawl to see who can live the longest, and whoever does wins!

Note: you're not allowed to leave the designated map area, nor are you allowed to build over the height of the walls or knock down any of the wall on your own. Doing so will get you disqualified, so stick to the rules and have fun!

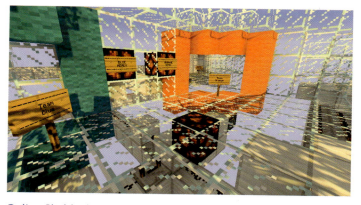

Online Skyblock games often have starting areas such as this, where you choose your team.

A typical set of Skyblocks in a competitive server, before the mayhem begins.

A Skyblock can end up looking like this awesome island by britishcommando2 after a long period of hard work and dedication.

SKYBLOCK

Skyblock is one of the more challenging ways to play Minecraft, and it is so much fun. Not only that, but it'll actually help you learn quite a lot more about the game and its rules, and it can help give you ideas for regular play that you might not have had otherwise.

Skyblock involves you (or you and teammates) spawning on an island floating in the sky that is made of very few blocks. Usually it has a little Dirt, a tree (or just Saplings) and some Water and a Chest with a few items in it. What's in the Chest and what's on the island differ with various versions of the map (of which there are many), but the goal is almost always one of two things. One- you complete various tasks by creatively and efficiently using the items and blocks at your disposal, such as create 20 Cobblestone or gather 6 Wool, while staying alive (usually you only have one to three lives). Or two- in competitive Skyblock, you want to kill the other players, who have their own Skyblocks nearby, and be the last player or team standing.

Skyblock is intensely challenging because you have to be pretty knowledgeable about the rules of Minecraft in order to turn the few blocks and resources at your disposal into more things. For instance, if you do not start with any Cobblestone, you need to know how to make a Cobblestone generator out of Lava and Water. Or, in another example, you may need to build out a platform away from your island in order to let mobs spawn on it.

As we mentioned, there are *many* variations on this game, and you may find one server's version to be very different from another's. We'd suggest downloading either the SwipeShotTeam's Skyblock Warriors map (bit.ly/skyblockwarriorsmap) for an easy intro or, for those looking for a true challenge (and an intro into a bunch of great mods!), the incredible Agrarian Skies (downloadable through Feed the Beast mod loader found here: www.feed-the-beast.com).

PARKOUR

Parkour is probably the easiest mini-game to learn the rules of, but one of the very hardest to master. All you're trying to do in Parkour is to jump from block to block on a pre-made course while not falling. If you fall, the courses are set up so that you have to start all the way over at the beginning, and if you make it to the end, you win!

Parkour courses can be anything from an actual mini-game set up with its own fancy map and server, maybe even with some Redstone scoring or other mechanisms set up, or it can just be a few blocks set up in a course on part of a map. Because it's so easy to set up, you'll find Parkour *everywhere* on servers, with many servers even building little Parkour courses across their spawn hubs or in mini-game waiting rooms.

Being good at Parkour is a bit of a badge of honor among Minecraft players online, and just about everyone gives it a shot. However, being that accurate with jumps is much harder than it looks, though with a little practice you'll find yourself getting better and better.

SPLEEF

The original big-time mini-game; the one that started the trend of making mini-games! Spleef isn't quite as popular on some big servers as it once was, but this is the mini-game that many of us think of as the official Minecraft mini-game, and it's still just as fun to play as it ever was.

Spleef is wild, and it's really not that hard to set up if you have a friend or two.

The concept is all about the set up, and it's pretty simple: a one-block-thick layer of Wool sits above a pool of Lava in an arena constructed of tough materials (such as Obsidian). Players start on top of the layer of Wool in the corners of the arena and use Flint and Tinder or Fire Charges to light the Wool on fire in the path of the other

players. When the Wool burns, it disappears, leaving gaps in the floor through which players can fall. The last player who has stayed out of the Lava wins!

There are endless awesome variants on this game, such as including permanent blocks to jump to for safety, incorporating a maze into the arena, adding Ender Pearls to the mix (to teleport around the playing field), using multiple layers of Wool, throwing Eggs (Splegg!) or shooting Bows instead of lighting blocks on fire, or even putting blocks of TNT here and there to mix things up a bit.

Spleef arenas have become so popular that they're pretty much a genre of structure in Minecraft, and you can find Spleef maps on some servers or on PlanetMinecraft.com to download. Or, you can make your own version!

Above: Players in a server match of Survival Games wait for the clock to countdown so they can rush to the weapon chests in the center of the map. Bottom: MinecraftSurvivalGames.net has some of the best Survival Games maps out there, such as this one that is quite reminiscent of the film that the mini-game is based on.

SURVIVAL GAMES

Perhaps the most popular game people have created within Minecraft, Survival Games involves special maps that have been created for combat. It's based on a popular book/movie with a similar name, and the idea is that a group of players start the game near a bunch of chests filled with various items. At a signal, all players rush the items and try to grab as many as they can without getting killed, while also attacking other players.

Like said unnamed book/movie, when you die, you're out, and the last player standing wins. There are *tons* of these maps downloadable online, and many servers that host them, but you can also try making

your own! When playing online, make sure you read through the rules, as the type of items available and the things you can and can't do sometimes vary depending on the server.

Most servers have hubs with portals like these, which teleport you to the land of the mini-game you want to play (Factions, in this case).

Factions bases can get intense, such as this one seen by Brewmaster_Luthor.

Over time, a basic little Factions hut can transform into a mighty fort, like this one shot by Phantomgamer.

FACTIONS

Looking for a mini-game that's a bit more long-term? Here's a goodie: Factions is a game that takes a regular Minecraft map and adds in the ability to join factions that can claim 16x16 chunks of land for their own. This land can't be built on, destroyed or otherwise tampered with (with a few exceptions) by anyone who is not a member of the faction.

Each player has what is called "power," and you can claim as many chunks as you have power (so with 10 power you can claim up to 10 chunks). If you die, however, you lose a power. If your power number goes below the number of chunks you have claimed, you will lose control over one of your chunks. You can join with other players in factions, which allows your power to be added to theirs (a player with 8 power can join a player with 10 to get 18 total). However, if any player in the faction dies, it takes one power from the faction's total. That means that if a player in your faction is killed 10 times, and your faction had 18 total power, you would then have just 8 power left. If you've already claimed 10 chunks of land for your faction, you would lose control of 2!

The goal is to maintain and expand the land you control while also attacking other factions to reduce their power. You can use special commands to join factions, or ally with, go neutral or go hostile to other factions.

There's no real "winner" in Factions, as new people can usually join and create new factions all the time, but Factions is a whole lot of fun to play over time, as you'll become very attached to your base and group. Things will change on the server, big attacks will happen and get talked about, and all sorts of other drama and action can occur. It's a very, very cool way to play, and it's one of the easiest mini-games to find on big servers.

From the Mindcrack UHC Season 16, this all-star team consisted of superMCGamer, oldGanon and Minecraft developer Dinnerbone.

Just about any amount of people can join in an Ultra Hardcore game. Here we have the Mindcrack crew gathered before the start of a new season. Many famous names in there!

Though there's crafting and exploration at the early stages of Ultra Hardcore, in the end it's all about who's left alive.

ULTRA HARDCORE

Outside of Skyblock, our favorite mini-game is Ultra Hardcore. This is a game with a ton of variations, but the central idea is the same between all versions: you have just one life, and you can only heal yourself with special, hard-to-make items (usually just Golden Apples, though servers differ on which items they allow to heal).

The best UHC (as it's known) servers in our opinion are those that have a decently large map with a world border of some sort (such as a wall, Water, a fall to death or a mod that adds a border), very few ways to heal and multiple teams, each using their own voice chat channels to communicate with their members.

When the game starts, every team will be transported to a random spot on the game map, and then it's on! You have to both craft and build up your resources (especially weapons, armor and healing items) quickly, but also watch out for and attack/defend against enemy teams. Whichever team has players left when all players on all other teams are dead wins!

It's a delicate balance, and there are a ton of strategies and competing philosophies out there on what makes the most effective UHC player, which makes UHC one of the best and most fun ways to play Minecraft for advanced Crafters. On top of that, it's actually a whole lot of fun to watch! In fact, we can't recommend enough heading over to the MindCrack YouTube channels (such as bit.ly/GuudeYouTube) to check out the MindCrack UHC competitions. It might sound weird if you've never tried it, but watching seriously good gamers play in a to-the-death competition with such intense rules is actually pretty thrilling!

OTHERS TO CHECK OUT

New mini-games are being invented every day, and so we've definitely had to leave the majority of them off this list. Here are a few names of some of our other favorites, if you've got the mini-game itch:

GhostCraft

MineZ

Rogue

Blitz

SkyGrid

Paintball

PLUS:

Civilizations · Annihilation · Bridges · Super Craft Brothers · Skywars · Last Man Standing

MINING BETTER

When it's time to slam a Pickaxe into some Stone, you need to be ready to go. There's gonna be a lot going on out there in your mine, from caves to explore, to mobs that'll attack you, to ore to snag and more, and it's easy to get distracted (and killed). Remember miner: when you put Pickaxe into hand and you set out for ore, you've got one goal, and that's to mine as well as you darn can.

To do that, you need to do three things: find resources, extract them, and return them to be stored in a safe area in as large amounts as is possible and as fast as is possible without dying.

To do that more often than you end up dead and far from your base, you need to keep a few things in mind.

All you need to mine is a good bit of Stone.

And soon you'll have something like this.

MINING

Mining is broken down into two types: clearing an area, and ore mining.

CLEARING AN AREA MINING

Just like it sounds, this is when you're not necessarily looking for ore; you're mainly trying to clear a space for a shelter or some other reason. This is fairly straightforward, but there are some ideas that can help you do this quickly and more efficiently:

- As always, don't dig straight up or straight down. This is the time when players are most likely to do this, so it's worth repeating.

- Cut out the shape of the thing you're making first. Designing a good area works best when you make sure of the dimensions before you start the heavy digging. Just mine out the outline of what you want to build and the rest will go much quicker.

- You can mine 4 blocks forward and 3 down from the one you're standing on without moving. Mining as much as you can in a straight line makes for more efficient mining.

- Stay aware. You never know when you might crack into a cave, Stronghold or Lava pit. Be ready.

- Take the ore you see. Don't let the plan keep you from grabbing some ore. Get ore as soon as you see it, then replace the blocks if you need to keep a certain shape going.

- Create stopgaps with Doors. Don't just mine open tunnels all the time. Put Doors in and even create little mini-bases, and you'll mine much safer and faster.

Some gold in a cave.

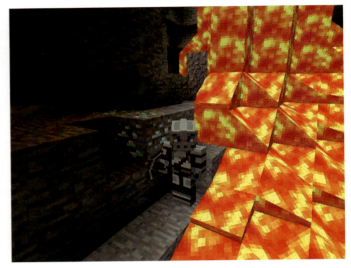

A proud miner stands by his Diamonds.

ORE MINING

This is the big one, guys. Ore is essential to Minecraft. Ore is what you want, what you need and what you will get if you try hard and have a little luck.

The Basic Idea: You're looking for ore deposits, and all ore is created right when you start your world. It's placed around your world according to certain rules and algorithms, and there are places it won't spawn, places it might spawn and places it's likely to spawn. Each ore is different. You need to know where each ore spawns and then look for it in those places.

Basic Techniques: Beyond just rushing into a big, beautiful pile of stone and hacking away at it with a Pickaxe, you should prepare yourself and have at least some idea of a plan before you go charging in. Try these techniques.

Prepare your inventory. Make sure you have most of your inventory clear, but you need to bring a few things for even basic mining.

Where Ores Spawn: Here's your guide to where types of ore spawn.

Ore	Layers Found (overall)	Most Commonly Found on Layers
Coal	Any level with Dirt or Stone	Any, but lower layers can contain more
Iron	2-67	5-54
Gold	2-33	5-29
Lapis Lazuli	2-33	14-16
Redstone	2-15	5-12
Diamond	2-15	5-12

You will find mobs in your mines. Be ready.

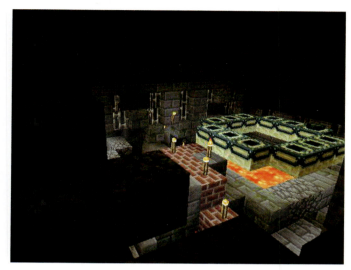

This mineshaft cracked right into the End Portal room of a Stronghold.

Bringing much more is not recommended, as you'll need your inventory full for things you pick up/mine.

- Plan out the location and length of your excursion. If you're looking for a certain ore, you know that you'll need to go to the level it spawns in. If you're mining close to home, keep in mind where your existing structures are so that you don't accidentally run a mineshaft into one. If you're going out to a new cave or area, make sure you know or mark the way back.

- Keep it tidy. It might seem like a hassle while you're doing it, but trust us; when you go back to an area you've already mined, and you didn't keep the excavation tidy and easily understood, you'll wish you had. You'll get a lot more out of mining if you clean up and light your tunnels as you go instead of leaving them dark and confusing. Make signs if you have to!

- Watch out for mobs. They spawn in the dark, and they will get you if you're not paying attention.

- If you break into or come across a big, new area, mark the entrance to your existing mine as much as possible. Light that thing up with Torches, because it is very easy to forget the way back.

A completed staircase to the Bedrock.

Staircase in progress.

ADVANCED TECHNIQUES

Once you've got the hang of basic mining, try some of these tried-and-true methods for ultra-efficient ore discovery.

THE STAIRCASE METHOD:

Most veteran Minecrafters will tell you that this is one of the best and most common methods for quick ore discovery, and it's easy to do. All you do is create a staircase from where you start mining all the way to the bedrock. Some players prefer a straight diagonal staircase, while others go for a spiral; either is fine. You may crack into a tunnel, cave or even a Stronghold on the way. If you can, mark this and keep digging your staircase until it's finished. If you can't (say, you crack into the top of a ravine), start a new staircase instead of trying to move this one over. The reason for all of this is that it greatly simplifies mining at deeper levels. If you have a staircase that accesses every level, you can head directly to the level you need depending on the ore you're looking for. Plus, it's very easy to see where you've already explored and to start in on a new area by building staircases this way.

The results of branch mining: Diamonds!

The branch mining hallway grows.

A branch.

BRANCH MINING:

Combined with the Staircase Method, branch mining is the simplest way to hugely increase your chances at finding good ore. It's also fairly easy, yay! To branch mine, pick a level at which the ores you want can be found. Typically this is layer 15 and below. When there, mine out a hallway 2 blocks wide and 3 blocks tall. Make this as long as you want, just make sure it goes straight. When you've got a decently long hall, go back to the front. Now, aim at one of the first blocks on the wall of the hall and mine a new hall (the branch hall) perpendicular to the original hall. This new branch hall should be only 1 block wide and 3 blocks tall. Mine it back about 7-12 blocks, then put a Torch at the end. Go back along the new hall and mine out any ores you find, then go back to the main hall. Looking at your new 1 block wide branch hall, move to the right 2 blocks, and make another 1 block wide branch hall off of the main hall, going back the same amount of blocks and taking any ore you find. Repeat this process on both sides of the main hall until you reach the end, then either extend the main hall and repeat or start a new one somewhere else. What this does is to reveal the most blocks with the least digging, meaning you're more likely to see ore with less work and time put in.

THE CAMP

Perhaps the best habit you can adopt for yourself as a miner is to never mine far from a base. This doesn't mean you need to stay by your home, far from it. We just mean that if you're mining and there isn't a Chest or five, a Crafting Table, a Furnace, maybe a Bed and certainly some safe, safe walls to get to quickly, you're mining dangerously.

Mining free, with a base farther than a minute or so away, is a fine tactic when you're out exploring, just starting a world or otherwise unable to invest any large amount of time into the effort, but once you've established a home, you should rarely be mining without having a secure area nearby in which to resupply, deposit gathered resources and hide from the elements.

Camps can be built just about anywhere, as all you need to do is build a small room wherever you are. Don't hesitate to wall off a section of a cave or build a safehouse within a structure like a ravine, Fortress or any other. You have mastery over this land, if you'll take it, and you can never really have enough safehouses.

To produce the best results, plan your mines by first picking a good spot for a mining camp/safehouse, such as at the bottom of a deep staircase, or built up in a natural structure such as a ravine or cave. Bring the stuff you'll need to build a good camp along with you to the spot you want to mine before actually mining, and it will make your ore collection progress much quicker than it otherwise would.

Well-lit tunnels are a must for any good camp.

Another shot of a good mining camp, complete with Chests, a Crafting Table and a furnace.

Camps can be as elaborate or simple as you'd like, but each should meet a few requirements: they should be secure from mobs (meaning they should be well-lit and only accessible through Doors or Trapdoors), they should be easily accessible from your mine (no more than a minute or two away from where you're mining), and they should contain a Chest with helpful items, a Crafting Table, a Furnace and possibly a Bed at the least.

Good items to bring to start a base include Wood of any kind (as well as Planks and Sticks), Cobblestone, tools and weapons, food, and Coal, Charcoal and Torches. Unless you expand your mining camps into more permanent bases, you should think of them as places to resupply and work temporarily, so transport rare or valuable items back to your main bases when you can.

This Miner has all the gear he needs to set out in search of ore.

Don't forget the Armor and the Sword when you go minin'!

For Mining

3 or 4 Stone Pickaxes

2 or 3 Stone Shovels

At least 2 Pickaxes of higher quality

At least 1 Shovel of higher quality

1 full stack of Torches or more
(4 stacks is a good number)

Enough food to get full from empty three times
(cooked meat and Bread are great options)

1 full stack of Cobblestone, 2 at most (partially
in order to make a Furnace)

Whatever Wood you can spare (a full stack of
Wood is ideal, but at least some Wood, Wood
Planks and/or Wood Sticks is a very good idea)

When First Setting Up Base Add

As many Torches as you can

As much Coal as you can

As much Wood as you can

3 more Shovels and Pickaxes of any type
except Wood or Gold

2 or more Chests

1 Crafting Table

Some Iron Ore or Iron Ingots

THE GEAR

A Pickaxe is all you need to mine, but it's not the only item you should take with you on your trips. When you need to mine, plan an extensive mining excursion that takes a bit of time and gear, and your trips will be much more rewarding.

Miners out on a serious resource acquiring jaunt should take as much of the kit to the left as possible for best results. You might not be able to acquire all of this gear at first, so just take as much as you can and improve your kit as you expand. Eventually, you'll be able to add to this kit and outdo it by adding better items as you progress in your world.

Each time you go out on a planned trip to mine, take the mining kit with you, and stay out mining until you use it all up or run out of inventory space. By doing this and combining it with the practices that follow, you'll end up with the maximum number of resources in the least amount of time.

THE EXPLORATORY TRIPS

As tempting as it might be, don't go just randomly mining when you find a cave or other structure (or at least don't do so for long). Plan your trips, get your gear ready, know where your base is, and head out with an area in mind.

- The best mines are centered around a mineshaft (a vertical shaft with a ladder) or a staircase that goes from ground level to the bedrock. Build tunnels or clear out levels around these, never going too far from the center staircase or mineshaft and always going straight out from the center. No twisting passages or changing levels, just straight halls, rooms and tunnels with flat floors.

- Keep your mine organized, but also collect all resources you see. When you find ore, follow it and mine it all out, but when it's done, repair your mine so that you keep it easy to understand. For instance, if you come across some ore that goes below the level that the rest of your mine is on, mine it out and then replace the floor so that it stays flat.

- Remember the two rules of ore finding: ore is most common below level 16 and near Lava. If you're really looking for ore, you want to have a base in the lower levels so you can explore them, and you want to look out for Lava. When you find Lava, dig around it, containing it as you go, and you'll more than likely come across some nice resource deposits.

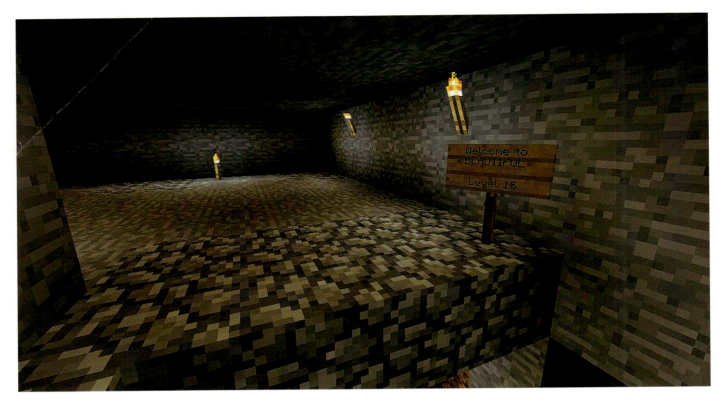

BEST MINING PRACTICES

Some general tips for mining, these will refine your tactics into well-developed, highly efficient processes.

- Use tools to breaking. You're already out, and though you might have some other project you feel like rushing off to, you're best served by using up the tools you have when you're already in your mine. If you take our mining kit with you and use it all up, you'll collect more resources each time you're out, making the time you spent in your mine much more worthwhile.

- Your mine should have a straight shot to the surface. We've covered this a bit before, but it bears reiteration, as it's so key to good mining. It should never be hard to get back to the surface from your mine, and if it is, you should make an easy exit for yourself.

- You should have a quick shot back to base when mining as well. Again, we've covered this but we're going to say it again: it should never take more than a minute or two to get back to a base from where you're mining. Keep mining far away from base and we can tell you from experience that a Creeper's gonna find you and ruin your day sooner than later.

- Deposit resources often. It's a guaranteed win when you take your resources back to your secure base no matter how little or how much you've gathered. Do it as much as possible.

- Leave no dark spots in your mines. No matter how small the shadowy spots are in your mine, light them up. You should never, ever have mobs spawning in the areas you are mining, and you can make that happen by using Torches and other light sources liberally.

· Use signs to direct yourself. Whether it's telling you what level you're on or that a cave or base is "This Way," use signs. There's never going to be a moment where you are sad that a sign told you where something is, and there will be many times you wish there was one to help out.

· Keep your tools close together in your tray. Switching between tools like Pickaxes and Shovels can take up a lot of time over many switches, so keep them right next to each other and you'll save a lot of minutes.

· Go in pairs, with one player mining and the other organizing. If playing multiplayer, split the responsibilities by having one player expand the mine and gather resources while the other cleans up behind them and keeps the mine organized. It really is worth the trouble.

· Leave a third of your Iron tools by switching to Stone for mining lesser materials. Use your Iron tools on all materials until there's about a third of them left. Then switch to Stone tools unless you find something that requires Iron to break. This allows you to stay out longer, as you can still collect the more valuable ores while continuing to expand your mine.

FARMING & ADVANCED AGRICULTURE

Runnin' around and a'murderin' mobs in order to get food, or making maniacal runs on Villager Wheat farms, is all well and good, and will get you through the beginning of the game just fine. However, later in the game, having to leave your base for food trips can get exceedingly tedious and frustrating, and it usually leads to a cycle of taking quick hunting trips that never gather enough food, leading you have to go huntin' again not too far in the future.

In the end, having a ready food source built into your home such as a farm or ranch is almost a must for a Minecrafter, and they really aren't too hard to set up. Here are the basics of farming, plus a few ways to kick your virtual food acquisition game into high gear.

The Tutorial world has a great example of an animal farm.

Sheep: they love Wheat.

FARMING

Farming also has two distinctive types. One revolves around the capture of animals to breed and harvest meat and drops from, and the other revolves around planting and harvesting crops of plants.

ANIMAL FARMING

Don't worry, this isn't about to get all Orwellian. Animal farming is pretty simple in Minecraft, though some automated breeder inventions can take things to a whole 'nother level. What you need to do for an animal farm is fourfold: find the animals and get them to follow you, put them in an enclosure, breed them and then harvest them.

1. Find and Follow: Most peaceful animal mobs in Minecraft have a certain item that they really like, and when you hold it, they'll follow you. This is ultra-convenient for animal farming, as otherwise you have to shove animals one by one into your pens, or just hope they walk in on their own. Here's what animal follows what item:

- Wheat: Cows, Pigs, Sheep and Mooshrooms
- Wheat Seeds: Chickens
- Bone (use on to tame): Wolves

You can tell that animals are ready to breed when they display the floating hearts.

A Baby Cow!

2. Put 'em in a Pen: Now that you've got some animals following, you need a place to put them. If you haven't built one already, just stick them in your home and close the door for now. Building pens is what Fences were made for, and this is where you should use 'em. Mobs need to be pretty close to each other to ensure breeding, so make a pen for each type of mob, and make them pretty small (maybe 8x8 at the largest, but more often smaller). Use Gates on each pen in order to get in and out, and remember that some mobs are hard to get in through a 1 block wide hole, so make double Gates if necessary. It's also a good idea to put all the pens near each other, and then fence around the entire section of pens. This makes it less likely that any mobs will get out, and it gives you a space to let some roam a bit if you need to do so.

3. Breed those Guys: Breeding is a necessity for any good farm because it allows you to turn your animals into renewable resources. There's not a lot of point in going out and collecting animals just to kill them, and then have to do it again, right? To breed animals, you simply need to find the right item to feed them, then feed two of them in the same area. They'll find each other, breed, and a new little baby animal will spawn!

Here's what each animal needs to breed:
- Wheat: Cows, Pigs, Sheep, Mooshrooms
- Any seed (not just Wheat Seeds): Chicken
- Any meat: Tamed Wolves
- Raw Fish: Ocelots/Cats

4. Time for the Harvest: Yes, they may be cute when they're bouncing around in your pens, but you need that food! To harvest meat and items from animals, simply kill them. You can light them on fire to kill them and have their meat drop already cooked (if they drop meat), but this method doesn't drop experience. Use a Sword, and take a few out. The key here is to make sure you leave at least two animals of each species alive so that they can keep breeding later. A note: there's no reason to kill Tamed Wolves. They don't drop any items, and besides, they're your friends!

A cool-lookin' farm on the side of a castle.

PLANT FARMING

The primary plants for farming in Minecraft are Wheat, trees, and Pumpkins and Melons. You can also farm Sugar Cane, Mushrooms, Nether Wart and Cactus, but these are the plants that you're most likely to need and to farm in your game.

Wheat Farms: Wheat is probably the most commonly farmed plant (it's between Wheat and trees), and it's simple to farm. Wheat requires a light level of 9 or above and what's called farmland, which is what a block of Dirt turns into when you use a Hoe on it. For best Wheat growth, it should be no more than 4 blocks from a source of Water as well. Wheat takes a variable amount of time to grow, but grows fastest under conditions where it's well-lit and on hydrated farmland. Harvested Wheat drops

0-3 Wheat Seeds when cut, making it a renewable resource. Use Torches or Glowstone near Wheat in order to make it grow even without sunlight.

Tree Farms: Wood is a hugely important resource in Minecraft, so tree farms can make your virtual life a lot easier. Like Wheat, trees need light, but they don't need Water to grow, so again use Torches to grow trees. The easiest tree to grow is the Oak, and the easiest way to grow it is to make a 5x5x2 space of Dirt. In each corner, dig a hole 1 block down and plant an Oak Sapling in each hole. Put 3 Torches to a side, and the trees will grow easily. Trees usually drop Saplings, making it easy to replace them.

Wheat, Melons and Pumpkins need Water and farmland.

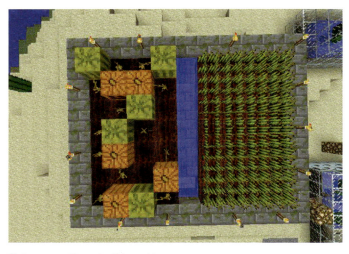

Set up your farm in this pattern.

Melon/Pumpkin Farming: Pumpkins and Melons are both farmed in the same way. Pumpkins and Melons work best on farmland with hydration, like Wheat, but they grow differently. When planted, their seeds make a stem, which when mature grows a Melon or Pumpkin in one of the 4 adjacent blocks. This means you need to leave at least one space and preferably more around a planted Pumpkin or Melon Seed. These also produce Seeds when harvested.

You can build an advanced farm by building it in tiers. By building the same shape of farm one on top of the next (leaving a little space between for movement and lighting it up with Torches, of course). You only need one source of Water if you let it flow down from one to the next!

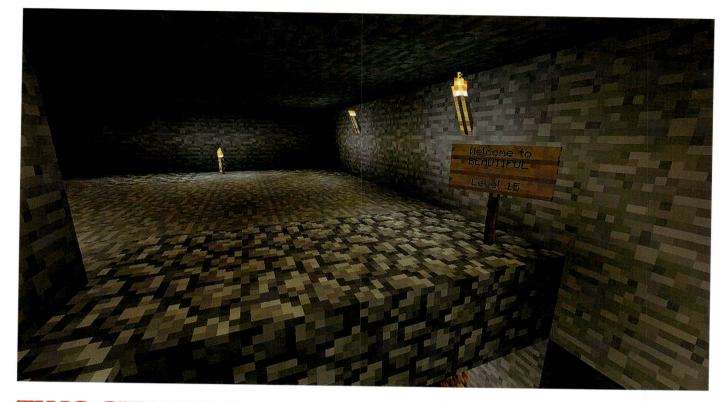

TWO STYLES OF AUTOMATED FARMS

Piston Farms can easily be attached to most existing farms.

THE PISTON FARMER

Pistons are one of the most dynamic and useful objects in the Minecraft universe, and when it comes to farming, they can help you out quite a lot. This build takes advantage of the fact that an activated Piston that shoves over a plot of grown Wheat will cause the Wheat to break and drop so you can grab it and use it.

This build can be added to most farms, but you'll need to leave at least one or two blocks next to each block where you will grow Wheat. All you need to do then is place a Piston on the empty block one block next to and one block above the block on which you're growing the Wheat. Make sure the Piston faces the Wheat, and do this for every block where there will be Wheat. Then, wire all of the Pistons together with Redstone so that they lead to one single Lever. (You may need some Repeaters.)

The Water Scythe caught in action as it harvests Wheat for you.

When you flip the Lever, all Pistons should extend across where the Wheat has grown, breaking the Wheat. Flip the Lever again so that the Pistons detract, and where there once was a Wheat farm, there is now a large amount of Wheat icons floating on empty patches of Dirt, and you can just run down your farm and grab them, replanting as you go.

THE WATER SCYTHE

Piston farming's fun, but when it comes to efficiency, nothing beats the Water Scythe. Like Pistons, Water that flows over a block of growing Wheat will break it. Unlike Pistons, however, flowing Water will actually carry the dropped Wheat with it.

By using both of these features, we can harvest an entire farm with the flick of a Lever and direct the flow of the Water so that all of the harvested Wheat gathers in one spot for you to pick up.

For this, you'll want to build your farm in a terrace formation, with one level of the farm one block below the other. Before you plant, go to the far end of the top level of your farm, and build a little wall with alcoves (holes) in it that line up with where the Wheat will be planted. Now, place Buckets of Water in the alcoves so that it flows out over the whole farmland, making sure that it doesn't overflow the sides. Test this out a bit so that you get it right.

Now move to the bottom level of your farm and see where the Water is flowing out. Build around this so that all of the Water collects in one trench that goes downhill and ends in one single block (without overflowing).

Go back to the top of your farm and temporarily remove the Water. What you need to do now is control when the Water comes out. The best way to do this is by building a system of Sticky Pistons, blocks and a Lever, so that when you push the Lever, the Pistons remove the blocks from in front of the Water, allowing it to flow (and when you push it again, the Pistons put the blocks back and stop the Water). If you don't have or don't want to use Sticky Pistons, however, you can simply use a block of Dirt over the alcove that you punch out when you want to harvest your Wheat.

Once it's all set up, plant your Wheat and wait until harvest day, which will be the easiest one you've ever had.

COMBAT

Thing is, when you play Minecraft in Survival mode, some creature at some point in the game will attempt to kill you, and it will succeed. We all know this when we start a world (which typically involves dying once or five times), but after a while you get comfy in your safe house and well-lit mine, and you forget that outside your cozy walls lies death. And then it comes for you, in the form of a sizzling Creeper you didn't see until it was too late, or a nest of Cave Spiders that you suddenly crack into, and you're dead. All your gear is probably lost, you're far from where you were, and then you remember: combat happens in Minecraft. Let's get you ready to fight.

1. PREPARE FOR BATTLE, YOUNG MINER

Nothing you do in Minecraft is more important to your success in combat than preparation. Every good strategy involves at least some of it, and it is the core of almost all successful offense and defense. Fail to prepare, or at least think ahead a bit, and you're gonna die. Do even the smallest bit of prep work, and you're gonna kill some mobs, kiddo.

So let's get you prepared. These are far from the only ways to prepare in this game, but they'll at least get you set on the path to tasty triumph over the dark forces that wait outside the walls of your home.

Crafter Robot Noise is decked out in enchanted armor and a Diamond Sword, ready for battle.

You'll notice the difference that Diamond gear makes right away. There really is no substitute.

Eat This, Not That

Best before battle:
- Golden Apple
- Cooked Porkchop
- Steak

Good before battle:
- Cooked Chicken
- Mushroom Stew
- Bread
- Cooked Fish

Bad before battle:
- Apple
- Melon
- Uncooked meat
- Cookie

Light up the area around your base. Hostile mobs only spawn where the light level is low. When you leave your base unlit, you're letting the mobs choose when to fight you. Turn the tables by lighting the area around your base, that way you only fight on your terms.

It's okay to spend on gear. We know, we know— you want to save that Diamond. Well, we get that, but trust us on this one. The amount of lesser materials you will save by spending that Iron or Diamond on good Armor and weapons is going to make that enchanted Diamond Sword pay for itself. You won't just die less, you'll die a lot less, and your ability to kill mobs quickly will result in experience and drops galore.

A miner's gotta eat. Food is the most often forgotten and perhaps most important part of combat. Health regeneration and the ability to sprint (and thus knock the mob back, aka "knockback") depend on your continuing to have a full food bar (the bar with the meat-on-bones). Eat foods that have good hunger-to-saturation restoration levels before battle for best effects, and avoid those with low hunger-to-sat. You should also bring such foods with you when going out hunting and eat them whenever hungry. Keeping yourself well-fed with the right foods all throughout your combat period is essential.

This pit and staircase combo is an excellent build for mob hunting, as it allows you to shoot from on top of it, drawing mobs toward you and hopefully into the pit. Make it even better by building a fence and a gate at the back.

Prepare the land. Make the battlefield your own, not just with lights, but with traps, murder holes and more. The thrill of attacking blind is great at times, but if you're looking to become a true hunter, take the daylight hours to prepare your hunting grounds for maximum success. Create pits, holes and cliffs to lead or knock mobs into and know where they are. Build tunnels and places to attack from above (little towers and forts) that you can access but keep you safe from mobs. This is where you can start to have the most fun with hunting (and essentially farming) mobs, and where you can get the most creative. Turn the area around your base into a place that invites mobs in, murders them brutally and leaves the spoils for you to collect.

2. OFFENSE IS THE BEST OFFENSE

When combat comes, and it will, don't go swinging blindly. And in fact, don't just swing. The Minecraft community has come up with a few tried and true methods that will amplify your ability to come out of a mob encounter on the life-having end by enormous amounts, and you'll find they'll lead to a lot fewer frantic trips back to your dropped pile of loot.

Sprint and hit to get a knockback. Attacking a mob at sprint causes you to knock it back. This is good for two reasons: It puts distance between you and the mob, and it gives you the opportunity to knock them off of something and damage them. This is especially useful when you know or have prepared the battleground.

Circle around while attacking: the circle strafe. One of Minecraft's two most trusted attack styles, circle strafing involves putting an enemy in the center of your vision while you walk around them in a circle, attacking the whole time. Called the circle strafe, this method makes it hard for most enemies to attack while giving you the opportunity to do damage. **NOTE: does not work on Creepers unless you're just crazy good at it.**

Flint & Steel Is, in fact, so useful in combat that it should be considered second most essential to a Sword.

Attack, pull back and draw them in, attack again: Kiting. Kiting is the second of the two sacred Minecraft combat strategies. "Kiting a mob" is when you hit a mob and then back away while keeping your vision focused on the mob. Mobs immediately attack after you hit them, so by pulling away, you can direct them toward you (as if you were pulling them on a kite string). As your target comes to attack, time a second attack perfectly so that they are hit and knocked back a bit, giving you the chance to back away again and repeat the process. Kiting is one of the safer and most effective strategies in Minecraft combat, and it can be used in combination with archery as well as with traps for seriously damaging attacks.

- **Swords aren't your only weapons.** The best hunters use all of their tools. Swords are the primary weapon, but you can also light blocks on fire with Flint and Steel, drop Lava, suffocate with Gravel or Sand (you have to time those just right), drown with Water and even slow mobs down with Cobwebs or Soulsand. Try all of these in combat at least once and arm yourself with the weapons you are best at using.

3. KEEPING ALIVE: DEFENSE IN MINECRAFT

While prepping and attacking correctly are great, sometimes you just need to stay alive to win the fight. And, let's be honest, sometimes you just need to stay alive period. Don't let your first thirty deaths get ya down, Crafters: staying alive can be done, and done well.

Putting a wall between the Crafter and the Creeper will save you over and over.

Putting Torches down while attacking ensures that mobs won't spawn in this exact area again (though they might be able to travel there).

This angry Spider can't get to his attacker when he's underwater!

Use the zigzag method. Most mobs do not do well with direction change when it comes to attacking (the Silverfish being a definite exception). Skeletons in particular just can't handle it, so whether you're attacking or running away, strafing from side to side will boost your chances of success.

Put blocks between you and them. Mobs will chase you, but if you make a move when they can't see you, they won't know you did it. This means that getting behind something and then changing direction or tactics can save your butt more often than not. This is great for attacking, but even better when you need to get yourself out of combat quickly.

Go underwater. No mob can swim to try and kill you underwater, so if you need to get away, dive down, kid.

Spam those Torches. Remember, mobs will keep spawning anywhere there is darkness, and if mobs have put you in a bad situation in one spot on the map once, they probably will do so again unless you do something. Spamming Torches on the environment when running is a great preventative measure for now and the future.

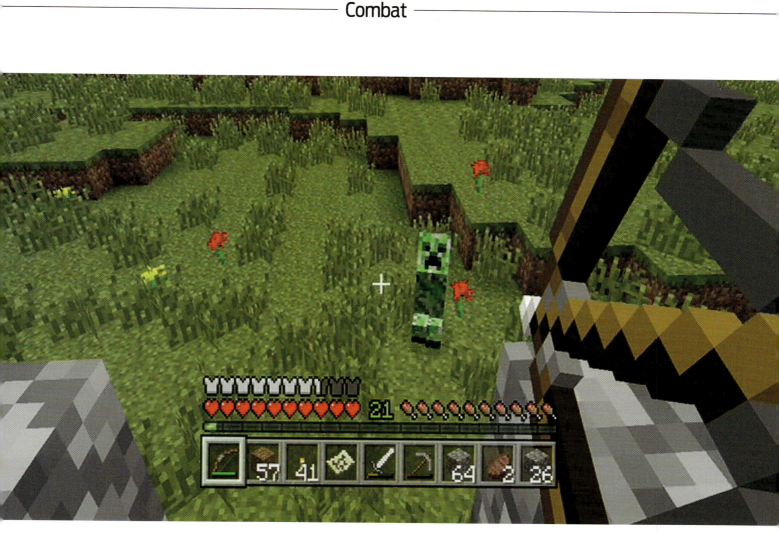

Any good general will tell you: always take the higher ground when possible.

With full health, this Zombie should be no problem. If this Miner was hurtin', however, it would be best to avoid combat in this dark tunnel.

4. GENERALLY GOOD IDEAS

Just plain smart things to think about when it comes to Minecraft huntin'.

Creepers start their countdown when you are within three blocks and end it when you leave the three block range. That might sound like pretty specific advice, but anyone who's played the game much at all knows that no other mob really compares to the Creeper when it comes to doin' damage. Know this fact and use it to your advantage.

Don't fight unless you can and want to. You don't have to prove your bravery in Minecraft. Fighting when you are close to death, don't have good gear, are far from home or are otherwise unprepared leads to death, which leads to losing precious items and time. Run away first, fight when the odds are in your favor, and your game will progress a whole lot faster than that of your "brave" friends.

5. COLONEL CREEPERKILLER'S STRATEGY CORNER

Okay we made that name up, but this neat little strategy section needed a flashy title. Pulled from the deep depths of the Crafter community, these specific strategies should be learned and used when you find yourself in a tough spot. When you get good at them all and combine them with the above tips, you'll find yourself wrecking your way through wave after endless wave of mobs, reaping their delicious experience orbs and laughing as you stand tall as the apex predator of the Minecraft world. Or something like that. NOTE: These tricks can be used on mobs or, if you're feeling rascally, on other players.

By digging above this Zombie, he has no idea he's about to die.

Getting past mobs in tunnels is a great use of the Ender Pearl (if you can afford to use one).

When a Creeper's coming head-on like this, the best option is to get around him and hit from behind.

The Duck and Swing. Best on mobs, make the mob lose sight of you, then move to attack mode. Basically, move to a place where the mob can't see you. They will continue to come at the last place they saw you, so you can move yourself to a place where you can attack them. Swing around behind or above, and you'll have the advantage on the unsuspecting mob. This strategy is super tricky in PvP, but it feels pretty great when you pull it off.

The Reverse Sapper. Tunnel above enemies or mobs and unleash your fury. Don't feel confined to the way the environment is set up. If you know where they'll be, dig so that you pop up just above them and rock them with attacks. One of the most effective strategies there is.

Ender Bouncing. Pretty straightforward, but expensive: throw Enderpearls to teleport around the battlefield. Especially effective when you throw them through throw walls of fire or where enemies can't see/ reach, gaining you a tactical advantage.

A Creeper's about to learn what the Pit Knock is.

The Mini Murder Fort from a distance.

Stack your Mini Murder Fort with some useful items.

Finn Fu done correctly is devastating.

The hilarious Sato Technique about to make a Creeper pay.

The Pit Knock. Set up a pit that's either deep enough to damage anything that falls in it or that has something damaging in it like Cactus or fire. Lure enemies near it and knock 'em in with a sprint attack or a weapon with the Knockback enchantment. Mob falls in, collect loot at the bottom, profit. Can also be made more complicated by creating a drowning or suffocating trap (see the Inventions section).

The Murder Hole. Create a border around a part of your base where you leave one block open just above where the ground level is on the outside of the base. On the inside of the base, make this spot accessible so that it is at your head-height. This will make it so you can attack the feet of mobs, while most can't get to you. Spiders, however, still sometimes can. Stinkin' Spiders.

The Mini Murder Fort. Get yourself all geared up and find a good spot out in the wild during the day where mobs are likely to spawn at night. Build yourself a little spot where you can reach mobs on all sides but they have a hard time getting to you. This can either be slightly up in the air or slightly underground (or both, for The Ultra Mini Murder Fort), putting you just out of reach of most mobs. Wait til dark, and then wreck all that dare come near. Even Spiders will usually just jump on top, and if you have a one-block hole punched in the ceiling, you'll have a fine window to kill them through.

Finn Fu. Start a ranged attack on an enemy with a Bow, then create a large firewall on a line of blocks in front of you using Flint and Steel. The enemy can't see through the fire, so drop TNT blocks behind it. Pull away from the firewall, shooting through it at the enemy. If hit, the enemy will usually kite, following you through the firewall. This will light them on fire, running them into the TNT and blowing them up. Works even better if you can put it in a pit and then escape out of the top of it. NOTE: Most items and blocks are destroyed by TNT. You will probably still find some resources that were hit with the shock-wave, however.

The Sato Technique. Set a TNT trap by digging down two blocks and placing one TNT block at the bottom of the pit. Put a block that can take a Pressure Plate above the TNT and put a Pressure Plate on it. Now kite a mob or enemy over the plate, and if you can keep them in the general vicinity, they'll go sky-high when the TNT detonates. Also works best in a pit. NOTE: Also destroys most items. But is really, really funny. Can also be used as a trap around your base, but not too close of course (unless you've got an Obsidian blast wall).

ADVANCED ARCHITECTURE

Now that you've been crafting a bit, you're probably ready to move beyond the basic house and want to sink your teeth into some serious builds. While the magic of Minecraft is that every person will find different ways to build their creations, we can help you in your quest to take your structures to the next level with these tips and ideas. Add your own touch to these, or use them in your own builds, and you'll find your world will soon be covered in unique architectural masterpieces.

One thing to note about Water Elevators is that you'll need to breathe as you go up it. You can do this by leaving space to the sides and sticking your character partway out of the Elevator as you go up and down.

Build little pool areas for the Elevator to deposit into (to avoid spills).

WATER ELEVATOR

They're not exactly the most realistic architectural feature you're going to have in your house, but when you need to go up and down a long way quickly and without having to spend a lot of resources or time building a Ladder or Stairs, you want a Water Elevator. Building one is about as easy as it gets: find a place where you want to be able to go from high to low (or vice versa) quickly, and drop a Bucket of Water so that it flows over the side of your high spot and down below. You'll want to build a little pool for the Water to catch in, and placing the Bucket of Water in a little controlled cubby at the top of the elevator can help keep it contained to one block (you usually only want them one block wide, bigger gets complicated).

This hole of Water looks unassuming, but it's actually an elevator that goes all the way to the Bedrock.

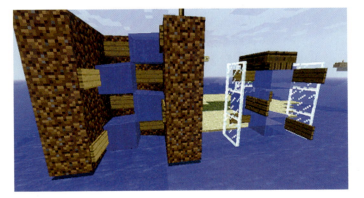

Some Crafters have experimented with different shapes and styles to create fancier Elevators, some of which utilize Boats.

These tried-and-true, well-used structures are awesome for getting to and from deep mines or high castles, though you do need to make sure that the elevator is not too long, as you will have to breathe at some point. Most Crafters have at least one or two of these around their map, and you just have to try one out to see how useful they are.

Note: Some Crafters make small one or two block wide pools on the surface that look like plain Water ponds, but when you dive in, they actually take you down to a secret base! Of course, if someone falls in or sees you dive in and not come back out, you might have an uninvited guest sooner rather than later.

Towers are almost certainly the most commonly built structure in the game, so being able to build one well is important to your Craftin' career.

STRUCTURES

And now for the real meat: the big structure ideas. Use these as a jumping-off point for your own builds, or try one out when you're bored and looking for a new project. More than likely, you'll find something to add or make your own with these, and that's what Minecraft is all about, young Crafter.

Start your tower by shaping it out on the ground with Dirt first.

TOWERS DONE RIGHT

Nothing says "accomplished Crafter with awesome buildin' skills" like a big darn tower shooting up off of a mountain-top, and they're often one of the first advanced structures that Crafters build after their initial house.

The primary thing to keep in mind when building a tower is that you should plan out the build a bit before you get going. Take a look at our tips on staircases above, and make sure before you build too much that you know how you are going to incorporate a way to get up and down your new tower. Staircase? Ladder? Water elevator? They all work, but they all require a little planning to do well.

Make sure your staircase is going to fit in your tower before you build too much, or else you'll have to do a lot of deconstructing.

Also, think about whether you want the tower to just look cool or whether it should have room to do things in. You have to build your tower's base pretty large to accommodate both a staircase and rooms to do things in, so keep that in mind when planning. One good trick is to make most of the bottom part of the tower the housing for a grand staircase which goes up to a single floor and ends. Build more floors above that floor, but use a series of Ladders to get between these top floors instead of a staircase. This allows you to have a neat staircase (always prettier than just a Ladder), a tall tower and some rooms to put things in.

Another idea to consider is to make your entire tower a useful, functioning piece of your world by making it into a lighthouse. Adding a bunch of Torches or Glowstone to your tower at the top will allow it to be seen from quite far away (if there's nothing tall in the way, like a mountain or Jungle Biome), which is very helpful when navigating the wild. Not only does it tell you where home is, it gives you a constant focus point, which does wonders for learning the land around your base.

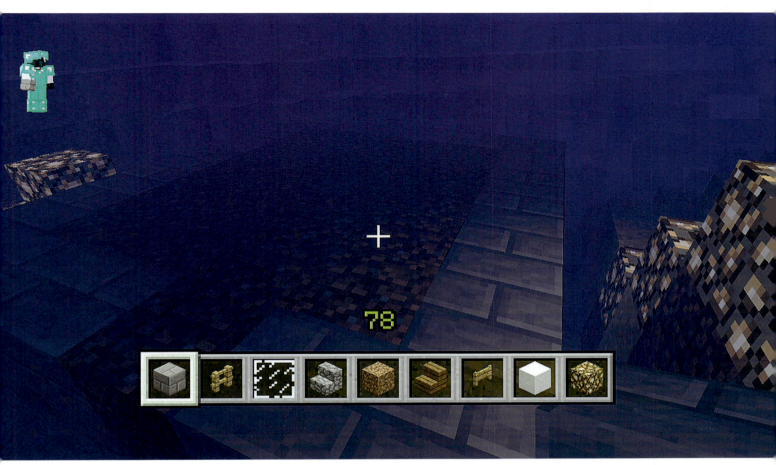

Make sure you don't drown while building your base underwater!

THE UNDERWATER BASE

Who doesn't want to live underwater, right? In Minecraft this is totally possible, but it does take some planning. If you swim down and try to just build some walls and put a roof on it, you're going to notice that your house is sort-of totally filled up with Water, which isn't exactly easy to live in. Plus it lets Squids in your home, which is just weird.

In order to build a base that won't drown you, you need to build the shape of the structure you want and then mine out the middle of it. Do this by making the shape of the building you want with blocks (fill the whole thing in as you go, don't leave any part hollow). Once you've got the shape of the building completed, put a Door down right in front of where you want the actual Door to be (so one block in front of your structure on the ocean floor). Doors are one of a few items that when placed cause Water to repel away from them, so you can then open the Door and punch out the two blocks behind it (in the shape of the Door) without flooding the space they leave with Water.

Crafter Darkscour took the underwater base to a whole 'nother level with this one.

Note how the Water does not fill the space behind the Door, even though there is space on all sides of the Door.

Once you've started into your base, hollow out the rest of it, making sure to plug up any holes you create quickly before the Water can flow in and fill the base. Once you've got it hollowed out, you can start adding things to it like you normally would to a base, and you can even make windows if you're quick enough to drop a block in quickly.

The primary problem with building underwater bases, of course, is staying underwater long enough to build without drowning. In order to do this, use the trick where Water will not flow through certain blocks that you can then move to. Ladders, Doors and Fences all leave at least some space around them that you can stick your head into and breathe, but Water does not enter the blocks they are on, meaning you can build little underwater breathing areas with these items.

Dropping a shell like this one from above helps you avoid having to be underwater without air for as long.

Use an outline like this one to make it easier to drop your Sand or Gravel

Another method is to use gravity-influenced blocks like Sand or Gravel to build the shape of your structure from above, dropping them down so they fall through the Water and down to where you want them. You'll still have to swim down and put down a door, and you'll need to replace the outer layer with something solid like Stone (or surround the whole thing and just mine out the Sand), but this method can make your planning go much quicker overall.

Below: This is what the tool at Plotz.co.uk looks like showing you how to build a layer of a sphere.

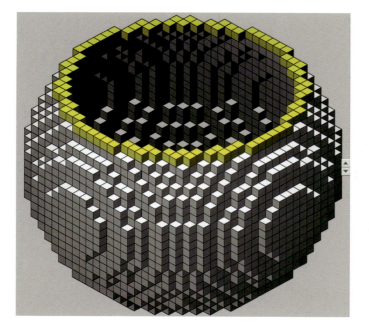

STRUCTURE TOOLS

Planning out big structures can be hard, and planning out giant, symmetrical structures like domes? Well that takes a seriously organized mind to get right without help. Lucky for us non-math geniuses, there are actually some really cool tools online to help you plan out your build, and they're free!

There are basically two types of main tools out there right now: plotting tools that allow you to draw out plans for a whole build, and math-based tools that show you layer-by-layer how to build complex structures like orbs and domes.

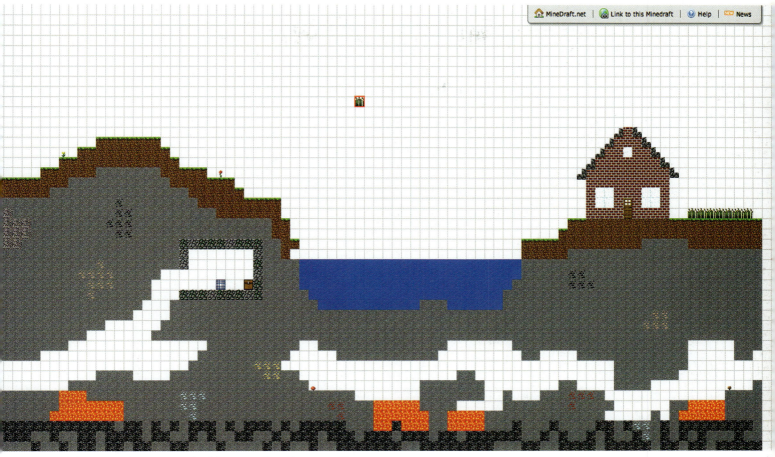

MineDraft lets you plan out your builds vertically or horizontally.

Plotz also shows you how to build a few random structures, like this observatory.

In the first category, check out MineDraft.net. This straightforward site simply gives you a grid on which to place representations of the various blocks and items in the game. Click on the block you'd like, put it where you want on the grid, and continue until you've got a map of your next build. Especially great for working out Redstone circuits, this tool is a tremendous help for complex builds.

For the more math-based tools, Plotz.co.uk is king of the spheres. What we mean by that is that it's a site that helps you build spheres and domes of various sizes by showing you what to build layer by layer. Instead of having to keep the entire, giant dome in mind while counting the blocks, so it ends up even and nice-looking, Plotz does it for you, and you simply have to re-create what you see on the screen. Your domes will never look so crisp and perfect!

Other tools to check out: Chunky, MCEdit, Tectonicus, MCSkinner, VoxelSniper

The BIG BOOK Of MINECRAFT

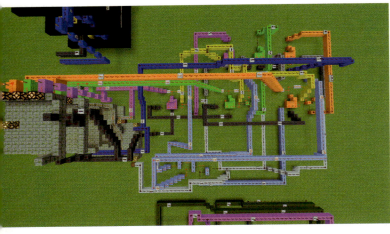
An intense Redstone invention.

Elevators are possible!

REDSTONE & INVENTIONS

If you've been playing Minecraft for a bit, there's a good chance that at some point you had to come up with a plan to overcome some problem or other in the game. Maybe you had to figure out how to pipe Water to a new area, or you needed to build a staircase in a small space. If you've found yourself in that situation and came up with a working idea, congrats! You just joined the ranks of Minecraft inventors.

WHAT'S A MINECRAFT INVENTION?

Only one of the most original and awesome parts of any game we've ever played! Inventions in Minecraft are pretty simple to define: they're things that people have built in the game in order to solve a problem or complete a task.

Most inventions fall into one of three categories: practical inventions, mob-based inventions or Redstone inventions. Practical inventions are all of those that do something that's maybe not too flashy to look at, but helps a lot in the game, such as infinite Water in your home or a mechanism that makes

Obsidian. Mob-based inventions are those that utilize mobs, usually farming them for drops or experience, but sometimes for other reasons like automated breeding. Redstone, of course, use Redstone, and they usually involve moving parts and lots of circuitry.

Here we'll show you how to make a few of the simple starter inventions. These are certainly not the only inventions out there, nor are they anywhere near the most complex. Instead, these are designed to get the ball rolling in your mind and give you some invention inspiration and skills. Try these out, and you might one day find that you just built an entire computer in the game! Make us proud, Minecrafter.

A bordered Water well.

THE INFINITE WATER WELL

No home is complete without one. The infinite Water well is incredibly simple, but it's also one of the inventions that you're going to find yourself using time and time again. It puts a pool of Water wherever you like it, and it will fill back up forever, no matter how many Buckets you take from it

All you need to build it is:

- 2 Buckets
- A space for a 2x2 hole

Make 2 Iron Buckets (takes 6 Iron Ingots) at your Crafting Table, and head out to find you some Water. The easiest place is the ocean, because you'll need Water you can pick up with the bucket (in other words, still Water or Water at the source of running Water).

Pick up two Buckets worth of Water, then go to where you want your infinite Water well. You need to dig a 2x2 square that's 1 block deep, or you can build one with blocks. Take one Bucket of Water and pour it out into one corner of the hole, then pour the other Bucket of Water into the corner that's diagonally opposite. The flowing Water will soon go still, and you'll have Water forever!

Make sure you don't get too close to the Trashcan!

THE TRASHCAN

Pesky, pesky Gravel and Dirt, always filling up our inventories! Well those days are gone with the newfangled home Trashcan. The Trashcan uses the properties of certain materials to permanently destroy items, ridding them from your inventory in seconds.

Get:
- 1 Bucket of Lava or 1-4 Cactus blocks
- Any space in your home

You can use any space for this because the size and shape of the Trashcan is up to you. We usually cut a block out where the wall meets the floor, then the block immediately below that one, and then two out from there. We then build Cobblestone walls on the sides of the trench we made, but that's just our preference. Basically, you just need a space that can hold the Lava or Cactus, and preferably one you won't touch or fall into (and that the Lava can't escape from!). Once you've got your space, just dump the Lava in or place the Cactus. Note: Cactus can't have a block touching them except on the corners, so you'll have to keep the area clear. Once it's set up, try dumping a stack of blocks into your trashcan, and watch them disappear instantly.

Bye, you creepy Creeper!

THE TRAPDOOR

Ready for a bigger build? This is one of the easiest Redstone builds, but it's still a bit of a doozy for those who aren't familiar with the material. Try this one out as a good way to learn the basics of Redstone. For this tutorial, we're going to show you the way this works in a space without any other construction around it. Once you've correctly built it, you should be able to figure out how to implement it in your shelter or other builds.

Get:
- 1 Sticky Piston
- 2 blocks of anything except Gravel or Sand
- 7-15 Redstone (at least)
- 1 Lever
- 3 Slabs of any kinds (at least)

Dig a hole 4 blocks long and one block deep (4x1x1). Place your Sticky Piston so there are 2 blocks between it and one end of the hole. Have the Piston so the green side is facing the end with 2 empty blocks. Now place 1 of your blocks on the end of the Sticky Piston (on the side with the green stuff on it). On the empty block on the other side of the Piston, put down one square of Redstone. On the block immediately 1 block behind and above the Redstone (outside of your trench), place a Lever. Pull the lever, and the Piston should extend with the block. If it doesn't, your Redstone connection is broken somehow, so you'll need to redo the previous steps.

STEP 1

STEP 2

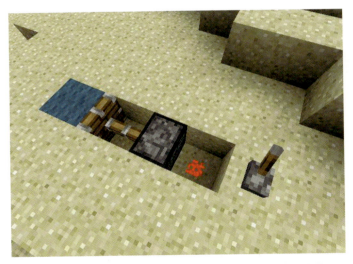

STEP 3: YOUR TRAP IS ON!

This method can be applied to your home's front door with some doing.

Next, go place slabs over the block with the Redstone, the Piston itself and its extended arm. Go back and pull the Lever again, and then jump in the hole at the end of the trench left when the Piston retracts. If you want this trapdoor to kill players or mobs, dig this hole down pretty far, or place a Cactus or Lava in it. If you just want the trapdoor to lead to another room, you'll want to build your room beneath it.

When building this for your house, you'll probably want to figure out a way to get the Lever inside your home. You can make the Redstone trail from the Lever to the Piston for up to 16 blocks, so get creative with how to put your Lever inside! It'll probably require some tunnel digging and trial-and-error, but it can definitely be done.

The House Cleaner in cut-away. See how it starts with a small amount of Water that is spread by the Stone below.

THE HOUSE CLEANER

One of the neater projects we've ever seen in person was a system that used Water and Redstone to clean out an entire house whenever a Lever was pulled, and this really isn't too hard to set up in smaller homes or those that plan it out from the get-go. When it comes to counteracting home invasions, whether of the mob or other player sort, The House Cleaner is among the best, as it's quick, doesn't mess up most of your stuff and can be turned off easily.

To build, start pretty high above the rooms you want your system to flood. Build a trench three blocks long and two blocks deep, then remove one of the blocks at the bottom of one end of the trench. Two blocks away from this, place a Sticky Piston so that it's facing where the block was, and then attach a block to it. Wire this Piston up with Redstone to a Lever in a spot in your house that will be safe from the Water, so that when you flip the Lever the Piston pushes the block it is attached to back into the bottom of the trench, closing the hole.

At the top of the other end of the Trench, drop a Water Bucket so that the Water flows through the trench and down out the hole when the Piston is pulled back. When you flip the Lever so the Piston moves forward again, it should then close the hole in the trench, blocking the flow of Water.

This is the kind of pattern that you should use to spread the stream of Water.

Under the hole in the trench, leave a few blocks, and then place five blocks in the shape of a cross (one in the center with a block on all sides). Four or five blocks below this, build a rectangular structure of blocks with holes in it every other block (a kind of honeycomb shape, see picture). When you pull the Lever and the hole opens in the trench, the Water will flow out of the hole and hit the blocks built below it, splitting the flow into multiple flows and widening it so that it can clean out entire rooms.

Building this for one room is easy (just make the flow as wide as the room), allowing you to turn the switch on and off so that the Water flows through and then drains out very quickly. Building it for a complex structure or your whole base will take a lot more work and will involve a great deal of planning, but it can be done, and it ends up being a very useful and fun addition to your build.

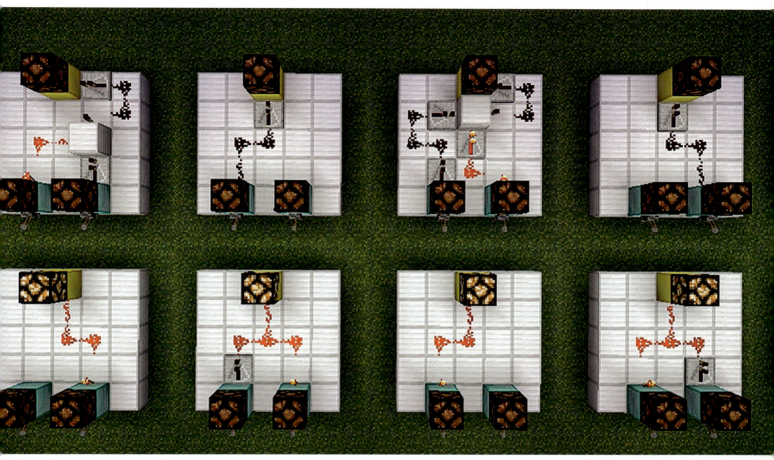

Most of the primary types of Redstone Gates.

USEFUL REDSTONE CIRCUITRY

The preceding builds are all a lot of fun and take a bit of Redstone know-how, but neither the builds in this version of Minecrafter nor those in the last even come close to encompassing all that can be done with this powerful game feature. Learning all of the things Redstone can do is really not that different at all from learning how real electronic currents, wiring and even programming work, and some Redstone builds are so complex that you literally need a degree to understand what's going on.

That being said, there are some fairly simple Redstone structures (called "circuits") that are essentially the building blocks for more complex Redstone builds, and by learning them and using them together, you'll be able to amplify the quality and scope of your Redstone achievements many times over.

NOTE: Interestingly, these "circuits" work almost exactly the same in real life wiring and computing as they do with Redstone, and they've all been around for a very long time.

The easiest Minecraft circuit to build, but also one of the most useful.

NOT GATE

The NOT Gate is the simplest advanced Redstone circuit, and it has a very useful function: it reverses the effect of a powered line. So say you have a Piston attached to a Lever: add a NOT Gate between the Piston and the Lever, and instead of making the Piston extend when the Lever is flipped and the Redstone line is powered, it makes the Piston pull back. This is incredibly useful when used on Redstone wires that branch, as you can make one Lever, Button or other such feature do different things to different mechanisms (like make one door open and another close).

To build the NOT Gate, put a Lever down and then a Redstone wire going out from it one block. After the wire, place a block down on the same line as the Lever and the wire are on. On the opposite side of the block to the Lever, place a Redstone Torch. On the block past the Torch (still on line with the Lever for this first one, though you can change it in later builds when you've got the hang of it), place another Redstone wire and then connect this to whatever mechanism you want. When you flip the lever, it will power the wire, which will turn off the Redstone Torch, leaving the mechanism without power. Flip it again, Torch comes back on, mechanism functions.

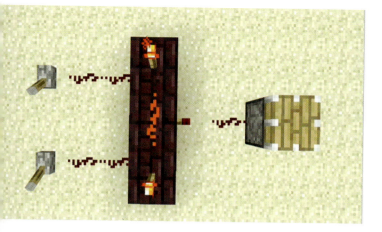

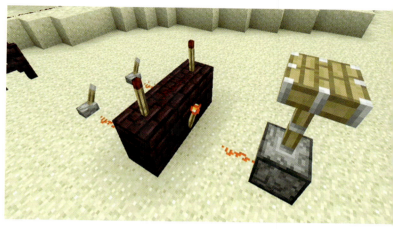

AND GATE

The second type of gate, and perhaps the one you'll hear about most often when players are talking about complex builds, is the AND Gate. Where the NOT gate reverses the power of a Redstone wire, the AND Gate is used to tell a mechanism that it can't function unless two power sources are functioning on it. This means if the AND Gate is attached to two Levers, both must be turned on for the signal to send to the mechanism beyond.

To build, start with two Levers set down going the same direction with Redstone wires coming off of each, also going the same direction (so there should be one block of space between the wires). At the end of each wire, place a block and then place a block between those two. There should now be a line of three blocks, two Redstone wires coming out of the two end blocks, and two Levers on the other side of the wires. On top of the blocks you just placed, put a Redstone Torch at either and and then a Redstone wire between the Torches. On the other side of the blocks from the Levers, place a Redstone Torch on the side of the middle block. On the block on the ground in front of that third Redstone Torch, place another wire down, and then a mechanism after that.

When a switch is thrown, it sends a current through the wire in front of it to one of the Redstone Torches on top of the blocks and turns it off. If both of these are turned off, the Redstone wire between the two Redstone Torches on top of the block goes underpowered, which turns on the Redstone Torch on the side of the blocks. This then powers the line on the other side of the blocks from the Levers. Turn either Lever off, and the signal does not get through.

OTHER GATES

There are many types of Redstone circuits and gates out there, with some of the most prominent being the NAND (NOT Gate + AND Gate), the OR Gate (functions if either power source is on, but not if both are), the NOR Gate, the XOR Gate and the NXOR, and all of them are incredibly useful for advance builds. In fact, knowing when and how to use these gates is what really sets the master players apart, and they fittingly can take a very long time to become good at.

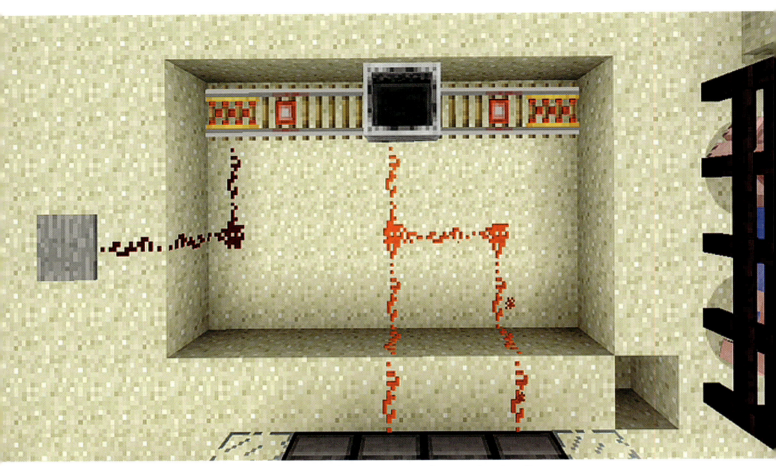

Want something to keep going off when you press a button? You need a repeating signal!

REPEATING SIGNAL

Rails, especially Powered Rails and Detector Rails, are also very important when it comes to building advanced Redstone circuits. This is because of the fact that Minecarts take time to travel over Rails, but they can also run over Detector Rails and thus send a signal, so you can use Rails and Minecarts to cause signals to happen at certain times.

There are many, many Rail and Minecart circuits out there, some of which get seriously complex, but here's a fun and easy one to get you started. It's a very quick system that, when built and started up, sends a steady pulsing signal through a Redstone circuit forever until part of the system is destroyed.

Repeating signals can be used for many awesome things, such as this wall of death that's about to let these Creepers have what for.

Setup requires that you dig an area down that is seven blocks long, one block deep and at least two blocks wide. Lay down a straight line of Rail in this pattern: Powered Rail-Detector Rail-Regular Rail-Detector Rail-Regular Rail-Detector Rail-Power Rail. Lead a Redstone wire from the Detector Rail in the center of the track to whatever mechanism you want to power, as this is where the signal will come from. Attach a second Redstone wire to one of the Powered Rails, and attach that to a Lever or Button. Place a Minecart on that end of the track, and when you flip the Lever, it will send the Minecart going along the track, hitting the Detector Rails in the process.

Because there is a Detector and Power Rail at each end of the track, the Minecart will keep bouncing from one end of the track to the other forever, hitting the Detector in the middle every time and sending a signal from it in a pulsing pattern.

This is very, very useful for automated processes and for complex Redstone circuits in advanced builds, and if you start messing with Redstone quite a bit, it's likely you'll find a use for it in no time flat.

1

GALLERY

Each and every week, brilliant new Minecraft creations show up all over the web, and each and every week we find ourselves "woah"-ing once again. It's absolutely mind-blowing how creative all of you wondrous little Crafters can be, and this segment of the Big Book is all about showin' off a whole new set of builds we found around the Internet this year. This time around, we think we've got one doozy of a gallery to show you fine folks, so let's get lookin' at some of the best Minecraft builds we've ever seen.

2

3

1. Sometimes the details of a build are so good they deserve a second look all on their own, like these inventive hanging tree houses in builder Aandolaf's Aandovale Grove.

2. Though a build should usually look pretty good in the light, Crafter Pixelbat shows here how freakin' awesome using the right kind of lighting blocks (such as Glowstone, Torches or even just Netherrack lit on fire) can make a build look at night. Try a night-focused build out, if you never have! They're super fun.

3. A combo natural and architectural build by CC_Architecture, this Derpy Dragon map is quite a lot cooler than its name might suggest.

1. Not everything built in Minecraft has to be a fort, a house or even all that enormous. Check out this tank entry in Kenny's Toy Pak by Aminoque for instance.

2. The insides of a rather fancy Redstone calculator by MDlolxd show that functional builds can look sweet too!

3. Mcholypotato built Coghaven here as an entry in PlanetMinecraft's Island Resort Project Contest, putting it in as a colorful steampunk resort town.

4. One very creative twist on classic Survival Mode that people have toyed with in Minecraft is to limit the player's world to a small cube, such as in Nefashus' Cube survival map.

5. Not only does this map called Steamshire Island, by lynchyinc, have a perfectly designed fantasy aesthetic, it also has a pretty cool backstory too. Check it out on PlanetMinecraft to read all about it!

6. There are few cities (or builds at all for that matter) that we love more than Eternal's Haven by Murps. The man riding an eagle you see here is but a small fraction of this mighty, and mightily complex, map.

7. Many folks have attempted builds of famous boats, but few have ever succeeded so well as this 1:1 scale Titanic by Deadkoalas.

8. When we tell you that when we loaded up ElectrickPickle's Eduun-Dragon map and this thing's head was like right by us and it made us jump, we mean like out of our seats. Yep, even a blocky Minecraft dragon is pretty freaky when it's this huge.

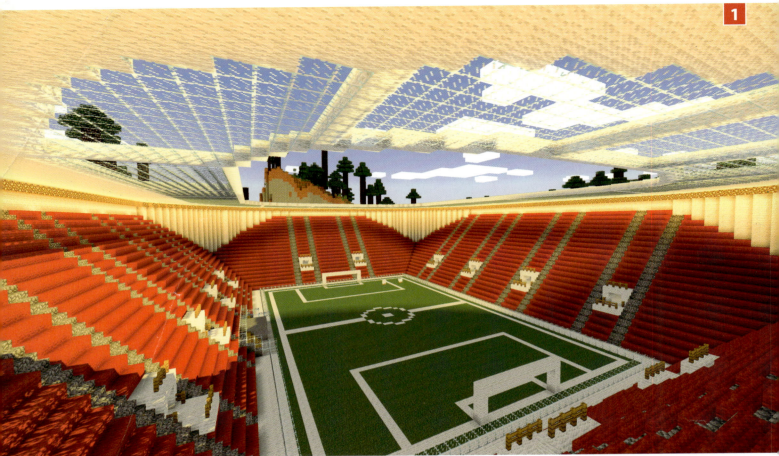

1

2

1. Sometimes simple concepts done well are the best, as is the case with this Minecraft Football Stadium by Avalanche_Ali.

2. Using shaders and the right map can cause some truly gorgeous images to occur in our favorite little game, like this sunset we snapped setting over the mountains of Gigorahk's Hub Terraform natural build.

1. Here's the same Hub Terraform build seen in the light of day. What a difference a few rays of digital sunlight can make!

2. Talk about creativity! This build is an ingenious take on the idea of an "A-frame house," a term in architecture that means a house built in the shape of a letter A. Builder superjerdotcom took this idea and turned it on its head by building a home not in the actual A-frame shape, which is based on a capital A, but instead used the standard lower-case "a" from the Times New Roman font, re-created it perfectly and used it as a frame for their home. Get it? It's an a-frame house! This kind of creativity is what really makes our Minecraft-lovin' brains happy, and it proves the rule that yet another time that bigger doesn't necessarily mean more awesome in Minecraft.

1. Not all amazing builds have to be downloaded: this one is used as a server hub on the awesome Lichcraft server, and as such is very easy to go check out.

2. Another by the exceptional lynchinc, this temple of Kredik Shaw is, according to the builder, "dedicated to nature, forgotten by time" and is inspired by the Hagia Sophia building in real-life Constantinople.

3. All *Lord of the Ring*s fans should recognize the city in this beautiful and mighty build by EpicQuestz (it's Minas Tirith!).

4. If you're looking to be wowed by as many creative builds as possible in a short time, the Creative sections of servers like MC Central are where it's at.

5. One thing that players are always looking for in Minecraft, especially online, is a good locking system. Luckily there are Redstone fanatics out there like mrian8ian8 to do the hard work for us like in this Lock System with User-Friendly Code Changer.

6. Building good PvP arenas is an art in and of itself, as zakmaniscool proves to a tee with this cool 12-Block Battle map.

7. There's an entire class of builds out there that feature modern homes, something which Minecraft's look lends itself to readily. Here we see P L A I N Modern Concept house by coolguy2563.

8. Night shots sometimes look the best. We think the looming shadow of this Pyramid by SirSqays that looks over its garden like a mighty guardian does just that.

1

2

1. If there's one Creative Mode server that we'd suggest checking out above all others, it'd be Treasure Island, where endless plots of creative endeavors have been built upon by some of Minecraft's best.

2. If you're a fan of *Attack on Titan,* you might recognize the style of this very well performed city build by etherealcat.

1. We're not exactly sure what xRoach means when they say this house, called Zen, is a modern organic home, but if it means it's a gorgeous home that uses plant life perfectly, we'd have to agree.

2. Once again, a builder comes along and shows us that intense creativity doesn't always mean builds so big they bust graphics cards. In this case, it's builder Cihla with their Way to the Future map.

1. Another view of Aandolaf's Aandovale Grove, here you can see that cute little tree home from the beginning of the chapter hanging in a lush valley with classical, yet fantastical architecture.

2. Spider tower! We don't know about you, but we'd be scared right to death seeing this monster by 8bitPheonix crawling toward our village across the desert. No Iron Golem's gonna stop that thing!

2

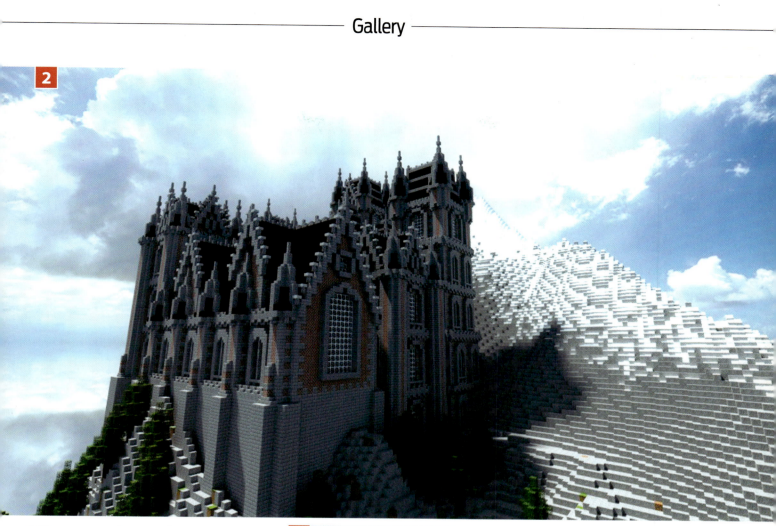

1. The awesomely named Mcgangsterhans slapped together this sublimely located 19th century mountain castle. We say slapped; more like put together brick by loving brick in a perfectly orchestrated bit of Minecraftian architecture.

2. With so many grey blocks in the game for stone, it can often be easy to fall leave color aside as a major building tool. Not so for Bataque, who built this crimson and cream floating skull island.

2

1. Who wouldn't want to live in a giant, super-high-tech biodome, we ask you? Well, whether you're down or not, we know that builder bobsajit thinks it's a pretty darn cool concept.

2. Sometimes a good build is brought to life by just the right render. This city by c-b-o truly shines when seen from afar, as all the details blend into something that looks like it really could exist.

3. Notice how the light falls so nicely through the windows of DSJDV's cathedral. This is due, once again, to the use of awesome shaders, something which we recommend every Crafter of the PC persuasion look into.

4. This is a build by TobiwanK3nobi that is downright huge, and it's appropriately called Giant Spawn Tower.

5. We're guessing that when Lizard_Bacon set out to create this house literally floating on a lake, they were thinking of a place they might like to live themselves one day. If you're looking for a new project to take on, this concept is a great example of a thought to follow as you build.

6. We are true *LOTR* fans, so we just had to throw in another shot of EpicQuestz's rendition of that most heroic city of all, Minas Tirith.

7. Almost anyone can pull off a basic ship and tower combo, but it takes master builders like Leopled1 to really turn those concepts into pieces of art.

8. Creative-Node here goes the extra step beyond incorporating Water into an architectural build and actually makes it the star of this excellent map, called Jorvik the Waterfall Village.

1

2

1. The Palace Of Daïbahr Boüiyait by schnogot is the kind of build that happens when people really study the architecture of real-life places for inspiration. Take note, Crafters! Real-life is an excellent place to go to for inspiration, so keep an eye out for images of things you might want to try and re-create in Minecraft when going about your daily business.

2. Taking an Asian turn on the traditional house build, nerdswrath created this Oriental Architect Plot complete with what look like appropriately eastern plants and aesthetics.

1. Fans of a certain green cap and tunic wearing, shield and sword-sporting, ocarina playing game character might recognize this palace by Kezsonaj. Just like real life, fictional locations make for excellent starting points for new builds like this one.

2. Or, you could combine the two ideas, using real-life building styles and theories to create your own fictional temples, castles and towns. Here Pandoras_Blocks has co-opted the Ancient Greek style of building to erect a temple known as Tempest sky.

WHAT TO DO WHEN

There's a moment in just about every long-haul Crafting session where you come up against something tough, and you're just not sure what to do about it. Minecraft is full of these kind of moments, whether it's deciding to stay down in your mine for another fifteen minutes before heading back to base, or whether you suddenly find yourself in peril and aren't sure if you should fight, fly or just throw in the towel and reload from your last save. While there are really no wrong answers in this game that's all about experimentation and playing how you like, there are some tips for certain situations that we can give you that can make your next mining trip go a bit smoother (by which we mean less full of death and woe).

1. YOU'RE LOST AND CAN'T FIND HOME (OR ANYTHING ELSE YOU RECOGNIZE).

We all love the goofy, blocky graphics of Minecraft, but we also have to admit that they can make it hard to keep your sense of direction. Since there are only so many types of blocks and environments, you can quickly get turned around both above and below ground. If you're stuck out in the wild and are starting to think you'll never see home again, try these tips.

· Get up high. If you're above ground, create a Dirt tower so you can look out over a bigger area, or climb a tree. If you're underground, stop trying to find your way out naturally and just dig up in a staircase pattern. Moving up is almost always beneficial in Minecraft when lost or stuck, and you can always go back down if you need to!

· Mark your path. Always, always mark your path, especially when you're already lost. Use towers, Torches, just about anything you'll recognize, and you'll start to weed out all the wrong directions (and will stop going in circles, as can definitely happen).

· Use the Cobblestone/Nether Rack "north" trick. If you look at blocks of either of these, you'll see that they have an "L" shape on the texture (on the regular texture pack). If you situate your miner so that the L is facing the correct direction (meaning it looks like the letter should), you are facing north.

2. YOU'RE STUCK OUTSIDE/UNDERGROUND WITHOUT RESOURCES AND MOBS ARE ABOUT.

Mobs don't care if you're ready for combat or not: they're coming for you. It's pretty likely that you're gonna find yourself in a bad spot at some point, with mobs a'comin' and no Sword, Bow or other weapons to speak of. What do you do?

- Get up high. Like with being lost, getting off the ground level is an excellent combat measure. Mobs have a hard time climbing even one block and most can't climb two (just Spiders), so put some air between you and your foes.

- Run straight through. Sometimes the best way to survive is to just put on a burst of speed and try and break through the line of mobs. If possible, eat something before you do this.

- Protect your resources. It's always easier to come back and find a Chest with items in it than it is to rush back to get the gear that dropped when you died. Bring Chests with you when you mine and store all of your important stuff when in a bad spot before trying to escape.

- If possible, build a mini-mini murder fort. Obviously you don't have time to do any major construction, but if you can surround yourself with blocks and leave just a little space to attack through, you should be able to time it so that you can hit mobs and they can't reach you. Very effective in a pinch.

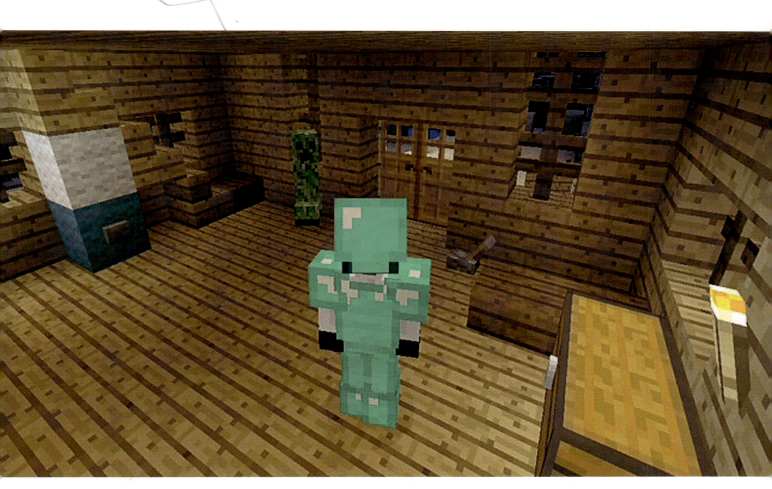

3. THERE'S A CREEPER IN YOUR HOME (OR PROJECT, OR MINE, ETC.).

It happens, sometimes a lot, and it's terrifying. There's one thing to do.

- Get out. Immediately. It's the Creeper's home now. Okay, not really to that last bit, but seriously, just go. While you might be able to kill the thing, there's just too much at risk. Unless you don't care what happens to the place, it's always better to leave and let the creepy thing see itself out or despawn than it is to risk having to put half your house back together.

4. A CREEPER DONE BLEW UP YOUR HOME.

But of course, sometimes you just can't get away in time. Creepers do be creepin'. But don't panic; you have options.

- Consider reloading. It may seem cheap, but so is showing up unannounced, sneaking right next to you and your beloved project and blowing it to smithereens. If you saved less than five minutes ago or if rebuilding would take more time than re-doing what you've been doing, you might want to reload.

- Take the opportunity to make it better. We all get distracted by new projects and tend to leave old ones sitting for a long time. It's super common to jump in someone's world and see that their bedroom is a lot shabbier than whatever the newest project they're workin' on is, as miners often get so caught up in other stuff that they don't take the time to update or upgrade their older work. If a Creeper knocks a hole in your house, well maybe it's time to add that moat you've always wanted! This is one of the greatest things about Minecraft: when things get destroyed, it gives you the chance to make them better!

5. YOU FELL IN A PIT/CAVE/RAVINE WITHOUT TORCHES.

Falling into darkness is hard and a bit nerve-wracking; it usually starts with a bit of panic as you wonder how you can possibly get out without light. But...

- Just dig forward and up. Hopefully you have tools, but either way, just put a block in front of you (you can always kinda just a bit, even in the dark) and break it. Then point up and break the one above it, and then the one behind that. Jump up and repeat. You will eventually either A) find light, B) get out or C) crack into another drop and fall more, possibly to your death. Whatever happens, you'll at least get out.

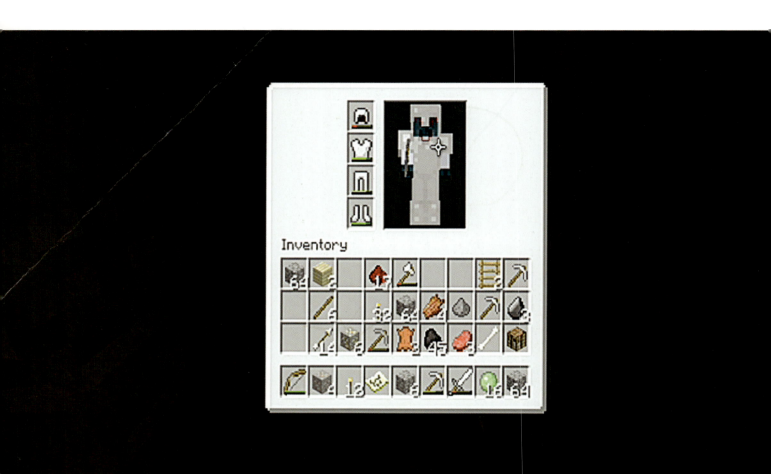

6. YOU HAVE A BUNCH OF RESOURCES AND WONDER IF IT'S TIME TO GO BACK, BUT AREN'T SURE IF YOU WANT TO YET.

Oh the many, many times we've thought to ourselves "I should find a Chest, but I'll just explore this one more cave." There's an answer:

· Don't stay out. If you're wondering if you should head to a Chest, the answer is almost always yes. Think of it like this: you just did a bunch of work, you have some good stuff, and you are currently safe, healthy and you know the way back. These are things you know for sure, right now. Give Minecraft the chance, and it will change one or all of those things within seconds. Err on the side of caution (and keeping your loot).

· Or, build a chest here and now and drop yer goods. You can always come back in a few minutes and grab it all, and at least you know it'll be safe.

· Or, save the game. Don't be afraid to use the save feature to your advantage. Hit pause and save real quick, that way you can load from right there and make a better decision if things go south.

7. YOU FIND SOMETHIN' AWESOME, BUT YOU AREN'T GEARED/PREPARED/READY TO JUMP INTO IT.

Abandoned Mineshafts are one of the more dangerous structures in the game. Don't go in unless you're ready.

Cool things are around almost every corner, and you'll end up stumbling across a ton of them while you were on your way elsewhere.

- Don't overreach. Taking a peek is fine, but if you don't think you're prepped for a big cave encounter, don't go down the big, dark, dangerous cave.

- Mark it well. Light the place up with Torches, build a big tower of Dirt, make a Flower path back home or better yet bust out a Map and write down the coordinates. Just because you aren't ready to go now doesn't mean you should let neat places and valuable areas be forgotten. Make it so you'll definitely be able to find it again, and then do.

8. A STRUCTURE OR AREA IS GIVING YOU TROUBLE BECAUSE IT IS GETTING TOO COMPLEX AND DANGEROUS.

In most games, you're pretty much stuck with having to navigate complex areas as they are, but this is Minecraft. We have better ways of dealing with nests of enemies, such as...

- Take the area apart. Just start simplifying the area by removing blocks and making it into one big room. You don't have to play fair; mobs certainly don't. Turn that confusing cave system or dangerous mineshaft into your area. Eliminate the threat by controlling the land, and you'll find that Fortresses and the like are just oh so much less intimidating.

9. SOMETHING INTERESTING POPS UP WHILE YOU'RE IN THE MIDDLE OF A PROJECT.

Say you're carving out a base, and you stumble across the entrance to a cave or a big deposit of ore. What do you do? Abandon your project and deal with this now, or save it for later?

- If it's ore, go for it. Get ore until there is no more, and then fill in the area so it is just Cobblestone. Your later projects will thank you, and you won't lose the organization of what you were working on.

- If it's a structure or system, secure the area, mark it, and come back later. There is nothing more dangerous than leaving an entrance to an open cave or structure in your base or project, because you never know what can come sneaking up out of the depths all the way through your home and even to your bedroom. Where there's dark, there's danger. Control the situation first, finish what you were working on, then come back and dominate that structure and whatever foolish mobs dare to dwell in it.

10. YOU CAN'T FIND WHAT YOU'RE LOOKING FOR.

Sometimes you start a game and crack straight into a Diamond-filled ravine/Fortress, and sometimes you go weeks on a world without seeing either. While it's never guaranteed to find anything in the game, there is a system that can help.

- Use the Staircase Down, Ladder Up method. Seriously guys, this method works wonders. All you do is create a staircase down to the Bedrock and when you're at the bottom, build a Ladder that goes all the way to the surface from there. Create a few of these in different directions and on different parts of the map, and you end up covering an enormous area in very efficient manner. You'll find ore, you'll find structures, you'll find mobs; you'll find just about everything. Even more effective when combined with tunnels, branch mining and clearing out levels around the staircase.

BEATING THE GAME

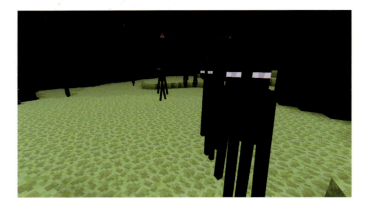

WHERE YOU SHOULD BE IN YOUR GAME

Most games of Minecraft that actually reach The End happen one of two ways: either the players collect the needed items as they otherwise play and get the opportunity naturally (which takes a very long time), or they specifically set out at some point to collect what they need to get to The End and make it a goal. It really isn't likely that you can play casually and get to The End, and even if you do, you are even less likely to do well there, as it is arguably the toughest scenario in the entire game.

You'll need the best gear you can get to beat Minecraft.

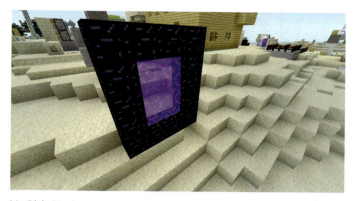

Ye Olde Nether Portal, ready to go.

Because of this, your game should be fairly well along before you attempt The End. Check off as many items as possible from the following list before you make your trip, and your chances at success will multiply.

You Need

- Diamond gear (as much as possible)
- Lots of Obsidian (meaning more Diamonds needed in order to make Pickaxes)
- The ability to enchant (requires Diamonds, Obsidian and a Book to make an Enchantment Table)
- Potions (requires a Blaze Rod for a Brewing Stand)

As Diamonds are the hardest ore to find in the game, and two of the other three items on this list require Diamond (and the last a Blaze Rod, even harder to find), you'll need to either set out to find Diamonds early in the game, or be at a point where you've collected quite a bit already before you can think about going to The End.

PART 1: GETTING TO THE NETHER

One of the primary ingredients for getting to The End is the Blaze Rod, which drops when Blazes are killed in the Nether. Naturally then, getting to the Nether is your first goal, and of course, this means you need a Nether Portal.

There are two ways to create a Nether Portal: either mine Obsidian and create the Nether Portal shape (Obsidian surrounding an empty space that's two blocks wide and three tall), or use Water poured over Lava that is in the correct shape to create the Portal. The first method takes Diamond, but a lot less finagling with Lava, while the second lets you skip the Diamond. We suggest going the longer, Diamond-using route however, as the benefits of collecting a lot of Diamond will help you out later.

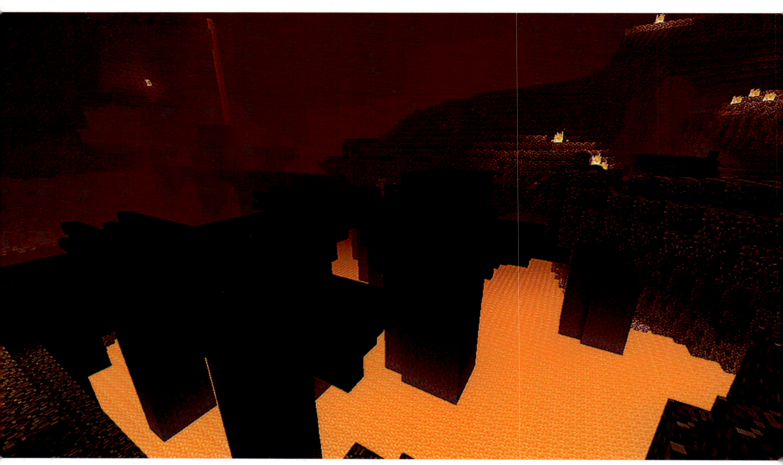

Yep, you're gonna have to head to the Nether if you wanna beat Minecraft.

PART 2: THE NETHER

Once in the Nether, you need to create a safe area that you can base out of. Though you can't place Beds in the Nether (they will simply explode), you can bring building materials. Cobblestone is resistant to Ghast explosions, as is Obsidian, so using one or both of those materials to create a little base is an excellent idea. It's also prudent to take decent armor and weapons along, at the very least bringing some Iron gear if you can't go all the way for Diamond.

When you're set up with a safe place, you need to start looking around for Nether Forts. This can be a bit tricky, as your spawn point in the Nether can often be underground, requiring you to dig a while. However, if you find a pretty big room, especially one with a giant Lava pool at the bottom, you've probably found an area with a Nether Fort in it. The Nether is much smaller than the overworld, so if you don't see a Fort close around your base, you should try digging straight, skinny tunnels until you find one. Another option is to create a second Nether Portal in the overworld in a different spot, as this will spawn you elsewhere in the Nether.

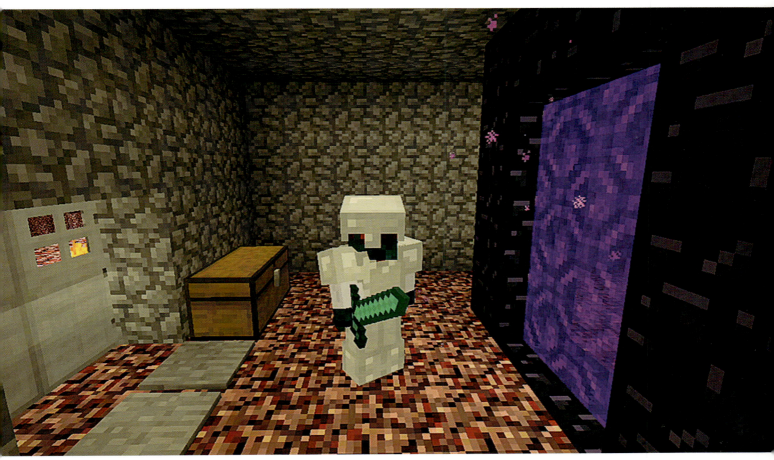

Don't leave your gate sitting all alone; protect that bad boy with some walls!

The Blaze spawner in action, plus a random Magma Cube.

When you find a Nether Fort, look for Blaze spawners. These are usually on little Nether Brick platforms at the end of bridges in Nether Forts, and you can see them pretty easily due to all the yellow Blaze flying around.

Killing Blazes is tricky. You want good gear, preferably some Golden Apples to resist the Blaze's fire attack, some Snowballs and some blocks to build with. Blazes can fly and shoot at you from a distance, so use the blocks to contain the area around the spawner, making it so they can't get out of your range. Snowballs do 3 damage to Blazes and are cheap and easy to throw, so they can be your best weapon against these fiery foes. Use those, Bows and Arrows and the best Sword and Armor you can make, and you should be okay.

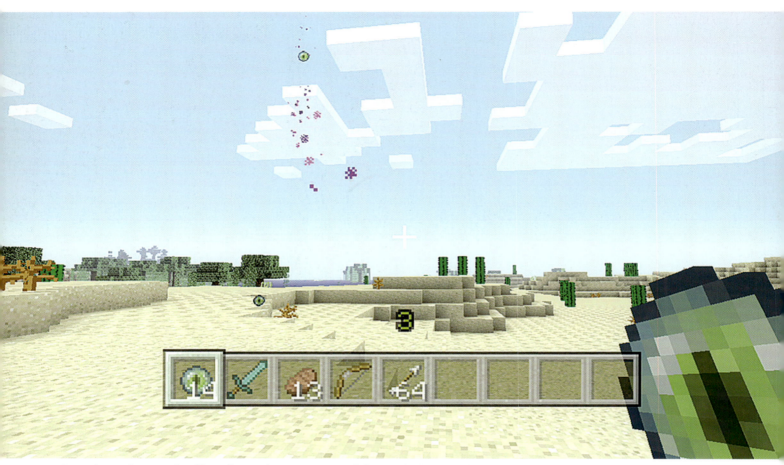

Note the trailing purple effect: this is what you want to follow to find a Stronghold.

When you find the End Portal room, you'll need to deal with this Silverfish spawner first.

PART 3: OPENING THE END GATE

To open the End Gate, you need to collect a certain amount of items and then find the gate. On the collection side, your first object is to get at least 9 Blaze Rods. One Blaze Rod makes two Blaze Powders, and one Blaze Powder plus one Ender Pearl makes one Eye of Ender. End Portals require 12 Eyes of Ender to open (at the maximum, some already have a few in them), and you'll need a few more in order to actually find the Portal. Additionally, you'll want an Enchantment Table, which takes another Blaze Rod. Add all of that together, and you need at least 9 Blaze Rods.

We've already shown you how to kill Blazes for Blaze Rods but you'll also need the Ender Pearls as well, which you get from killing Endermen. This is when the Kill More Mobs section of this guide will come in handy, and you'll probably have to kill quite a few as they don't always drop the Pearls. You should collect at least 16 Ender Pearls, and 20 is even safer.

A nice little End Gate base.

Give your Portal base everything you can, especially a Bed. You'll probably be dying a few times, so you'll be back here soon.

Once you have your Rods and have made them into Powder (leaving one for your Enchantment Table) and have combined the Powder with the Pearls to make Eyes of Ender, you need to find a Stronghold. This is where your extra Eyes come into play: throw your Eyes of Ender, and they will shoot out toward a Stronghold. You may be able to pick up the Eye again, but they can also break so be careful about not throwing too many (make sure you keep at least 12).

Follow the Eyes, and eventually you'll get to a Stronghold. You'll have to explore the Stronghold, but somewhere in it you will find a room with Lava, a Nether Portal and some Silverfish blocks. Make sure to kill and contain the Silverfish, then build a containment area/mini-base around the Portal. Finally, activate it by placing the Eyes of Ender into the Portal blocks, and you'll see it kick on!

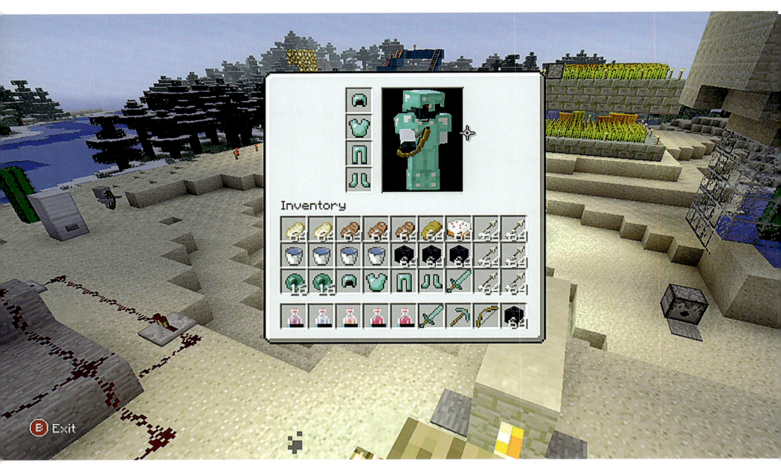

This miner is well decked out to do some major damage to the Ender Dragon.

PART 4: PREP

Now hold yer horses young Crafter: you need to get ready before you dive through that Portal. Besides getting all the best gear you can, you also need to do a few more things before you make the plunge.

- Get the area around your Portal ready. If you die in The End, you just go back to your spawn point in the overworld. Make that mini-base around your Portal and include a Bed that you've slept in and Chests with tons of gear in them. This way when you die, you just gear up again and head right back to The End.

- Take the best gear, and enchant as much of it as is possible.

- In addition to a Diamond Sword or two, bring a Bow and as many Arrows as you can.

- Also bring Potions, a Pumpkin (to wear if the Endermen bother you too much), Water Buckets (to scare off the Endermen), Obsidian, Ladders, Chests and food. This is your kit to beat The End.

Once you've got your base prepared and have everything you need, you're ready to go wreck you an Ender Dragon. **Whoo!**

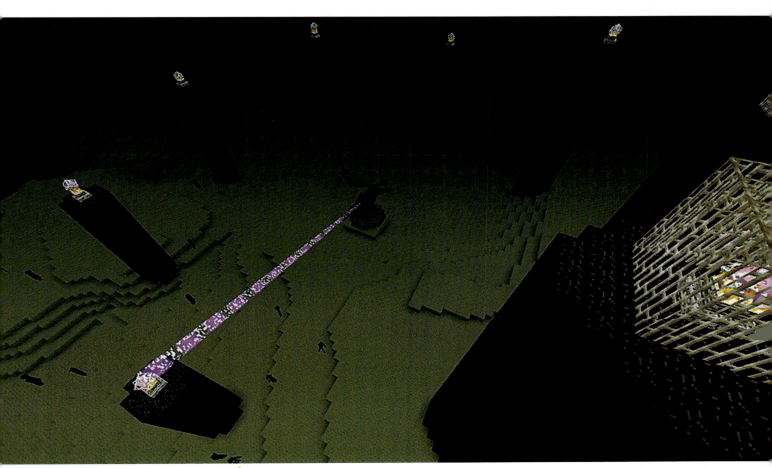

The Ender Dragon is a tough foe, but he can be beat with a little skill and a little luck..

PART 5: DEALING WITH THE END

You'll notice right off the bat that The End is different from the other areas. First thing's first: you need to get off the little area you're floating on and over to the main island. Use Obsidian to build a bridge over, and be careful! The main island is covered in Endermen, not to mention that big ole Ender Dragon flying around.

You can always go straight to the attack, but this isn't likely to get you anywhere but dead unless you are just insanely geared up and good at combat. The best bet for survival and success is, as we so often say in Minecrafter, to control the area.

Use your Obsidian to build yourself a small fort or safe area in The End. Make this so that Endermen can't get in and the Ender Dragon can't see you (so you'll need to make a few layers within it, or some entrance passageways that twist and are too small for the Endermen to get through). The Dragon can't break Obsidian, so you'll be relatively safe to put down resupply Chests in your Obsidian fort, as well as to use it to shoot at your enemies.

Endermen are mostly just pests in The End, so it's best just to kill them quickly or avoid them altogether. Use your Buckets of Water and Pumpkin for this (Endermen won't see you with a Pumpkin on your head, and they hate and are damaged by Water).

Shoot these crystal, Dragon-charger things with arrows if possible, as they explode.

PART 6: KILLING THE ENDER DRAGON

Building an Obsidian fort and messin' with Endermen is pretty fun, but you're here for one reason: to kill that big darn Dragon. You'll notice that beams are flying out of those giant Obsidian pillars and touching the Dragon as he flies around: these come out of crystals on the tops of the pillars, and they heal the Dragon. You can't kill him with these still going, as he'll just heal, so you need to take them out.

There are two common methods for this: shoot out the crystals from below with a Bow or Snowballs, or climb the pillars and break the crystals with a Sword.

Either method works, though you'll have to be a good shot for the first, and you'll have to deal with the crystals exploding when broken for the second.

Once the crystals are out, attack the Dragon. Enchanted Bows are probably the best weapon here, as you can hit the Dragon when flying, but you can use just about any combat method you want. The keys here are these: have a big supply of the best gear you can get, avoid the fire blasts (they're pretty slow), hide when you need to (in fact, staying in your base and shooting out of it is a great method), and use items like food and potions to keep your health and strength up constantly.

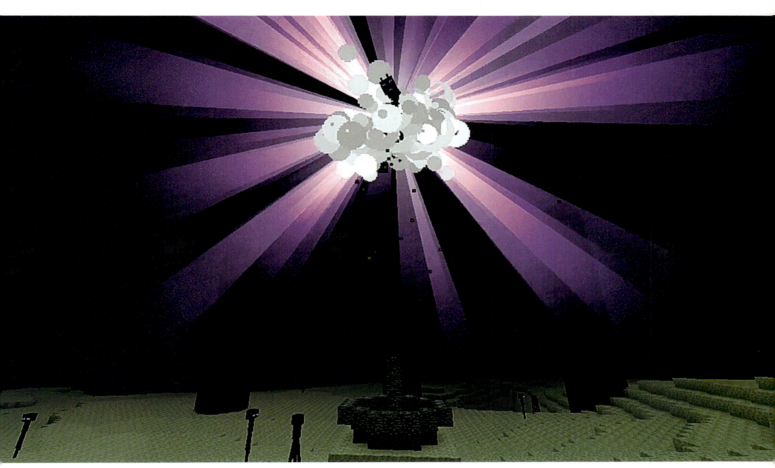

When you finally kill that bad boy Dragon, you'll be rewarded with one of the coolest sights in Minecraft.

A crystal shatters from a bow shot.

It will be expensive, you will die a lot, and it will take a long time. But when you finally see that health bar drop to nil, and the Dragon starts exploding light everywhere and dropping the craziest amount of experience you've ever seen, you'll know it was all worth it. You've just "beat" Minecraft, brave young Crafter!

Note: Make sure to read the infamous "End Poem" after killing the Ender Dragon. It's a very cool piece of writing, and it'll make you see the game in a different light! It's also one of the only actual "story" parts in the game, so be sure not to miss it.

OTHER BUILDING & SANDBOX GAMES

Minecraft is without a doubt the most popular sandbox building game of all time, but it definitely isn't the only such game out there. From the games that inspired Minecraft to games inspired by Minecraft to building games that have nothing to do with our favorite block-based builder, sandbox building is a big and varied genre full of incredibly fun video games.

Each of these games has something in common with Minecraft, whether it's building, exploration or survival, but each brings its own twists and unique features with it, such as Starbound's focus on interstellar travel, or Block Fortress' tower defense style of play. If you're looking to expand your building options and maybe find another game to obsess about, look no further.

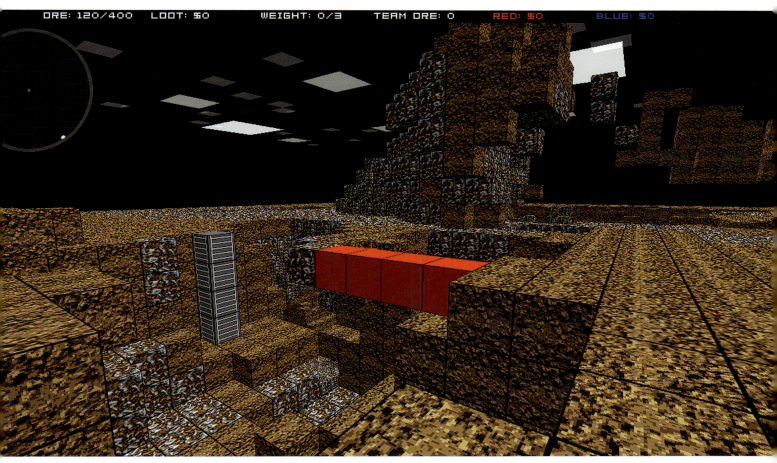

It's easy to see how this game influenced Minecraft.

Infiniminer uses a class system, unlike Minecraft.

INFINIMINER

Another Minecraft inspiration, Infiniminer is where Minecraft got its use of blocks and the idea of mining resources and building things with them. Unfortunately, the source code for Infiniminer was leaked soon after its creation, and people started making their own versions and mods for the game. This made it impossible for the creator to keep updating it, so development was quickly stopped.

Because it's very similar to Minecraft, there's not a whole lot to say about Infiniminer, but we mention it as a nod to those that paved the way for our favorite game. If you feel like playing a bit of gaming history, you can still get the files from the Zachtronics Industries website.

Cube World features gorgeous landscapes, full of plenty to do...

...epic combat and much, much more.

CUBE WORLD

If you always wished that Minecraft had more RPG elements to it, such as classes, races, spells, more weapons and extended combat, you'll wanna check out Cube World. Cube World is a block-based fantasy adventure game that puts the focus on killing monsters and exploring in order to find more monsters to slay.

Cube World resembles Minecraft in that it uses blocks to create everything and terrain is destroyable, but the building function isn't done yet, so there's no house creation. What is there is a gorgeous game, admittedly prettier than Minecraft, which has absolutely tons to do in terms of role playing, adventuring and bad-guy slaying. It looks and feels a little like later Zelda games if Zelda was set in a Minecraft-like world. Of the sandbox builders in progress, this is one of the best put-together.

Ace of Spades lets you blow people up *and* build.

ACE OF SPADES

If Cube World is Minecraft-meets-Zelda, Ace of Spades is Minecraft meets the online first person shooter. It combines the idea of building and digging in a block-based world with typical FPS combat matches, such as "capture the flag," "team deathmatch" and defensive modes.

Like most FPS games, Ace of Spades has a class system and multiple weapon choices, but deciding which class and items you carry also depends on whether or not you plan on building or mining. The idea is that some players will create forts and other defenses for their team while helping out with the combat when they can, while others focus more on killing. Additionally, mining can be used offensively to take down or sneak into enemy bases.

Maps on Ace of Spades can be randomly generated or player-created, and they look great, usually complete with epic terrain and nicely built structures and cities. Ace of Spades is a very, very different experience from Minecraft and most other block builders despite its similarities, making it one of the most notable Minecraft-related games out there.

They call it "side-scroller Minecraft," but Starbound and Terraria are oh so much more than that.

STARBOUND
[Windows, OS X, Linux, Console versions TBA]

We don't like to play favorites with our games, but we gotta tell you Crafters, there have been few games in the past few years that we've been more excited about than Starbound. Those who are familiar with the excellent game Terraria will notice right off the bat that Starbound looks a bit like Terraria in space, and that's not far off the mark. Starbound is a side-scrolling adventure builder, just like Terraria, and in fact it's created by the same people and has a similar feel to its look and controls.

Unlike Terarria, however, Starbound is set in space and your character is not stuck to a single world. Instead,

you live in a starship (which you can modify and build on) that can fly between various planets, which you can beam down to for exploration, building, resource-collection and, of course, battle. You can also choose from a variety of races, from fish people to the robot folk named "The Glitch," and each race has its own worlds, looks and even building styles, which when combined together makes for some darn cool builds.

Starbound takes the great parts of Terraria and builds on them, and the freedom of being able to go from planet to planet gives the concept an openness and boost of fun that few games in the builder genre have yet matched. Starbound is just getting started, but it's only gotten better with each update.

Like in many builder games, bases are a big deal in Terraria.

TERRARIA

[Windows, PlayStation 3, Xbox 360, PlayStation Vita, iOS, Android]

Speaking of Terraria, we talked about this gorgeous side-scrolling, pixel-happy game in our last Minecraft book, but we have to bring it back up because it has just continued to get better and better. After stating that they were not going to update the game after January 2012, Terraria creators Re-Logic saw a huge number of fans swarm to their game during 2013, and by October they were back to putting out great new content for this beloved game.

And by putting out content, we mean a lot of content. In fact, Terraria has seen nine new updates since October 2013, and the amount of content added is staggering. From dozens of new mobs and items to updates to combat, building and even the way the game looks Terraria is currently leading the pack when it comes to builder alternatives to Minecraft, and it's basically a whole new game from what it was this time last year. We cannot recommend this game enough, and it looks like they plan on continuing to update it for a good long while.

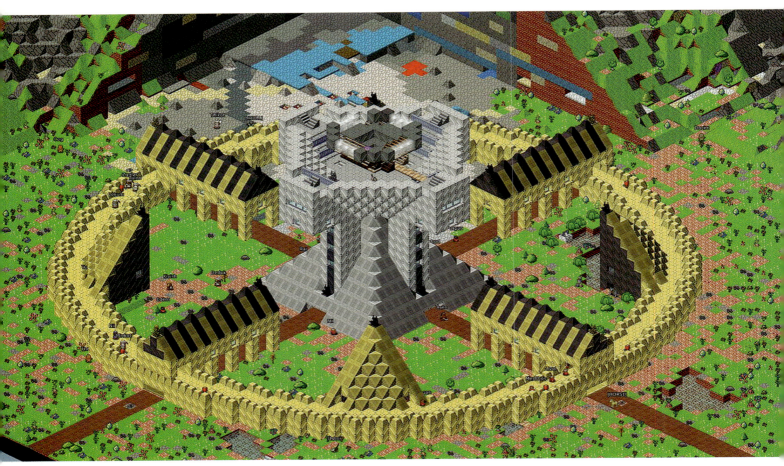

A gorgeous dwarf-filled fortress.

Another visual mod for the game.

DWARF FORTRESS

Here's the thing about Dwarf Fortress: finding a gamer that's heard of Dwarf Fortress isn't super hard, and if you find one that has, there's a pretty good chance that they respect this quirky game. However, finding someone who's actually played Dwarf Fortress is a whole lot harder, and finding someone who's good at Dwarf Fortress...well, let's just say it isn't something that happens to most people in a lifetime.

Dwarf Fortress is one of the inspirations for Minecraft, and it's also one of the hardest video games of all time. On top of that, it's one of the strangest-looking games of all time as well, and its difficulty is largely tied into the way it looks. Dwarf Fortress is what's called an ASCII game, ASCII being a coding system that uses codes and characters based on the English alphabet. Essentially, it's the symbols your keyboard can make, and those are exactly what every single thing in Dwarf Fortress is made from.

Dwarf Fortress can be modified to have better visuals.

That might not seem too complex, until you understand that there are hundreds of different creatures, characters, environments, objects, plants, structures and more in Dwarf Fortress, each of which is represented only by ASCII characters (so keyboard characters).

It's partly what's called a "roguelike" game, which basically means that you control characters in a randomly generated world in which death is just one of many possible events. In Dwarf Fortress' case, this is especially true, as the game generates an entire world, including continents and a huge variety of terrain and environment types.

Your goal in Dwarf Fortress is straightforward: take control of a group of dwarves and try to help them thrive and survive. You do this by giving dwarves tasks, such as mining, cooking or building a mountain fortress. As we mentioned, Dwarf Fortress is one of the most complex games ever, so the list of things your dwarves can do or that can happen is enormous, as are the mind-boggling backstories and histories of each randomly generated game.

Be warned: Dwarf Fortress makes no pretention of players being even remotely capable of keeping their fort alive and prospering forever. There's no way to "beat" Dwarf Fortress, and in fact the motto of the game is "Losing is fun."

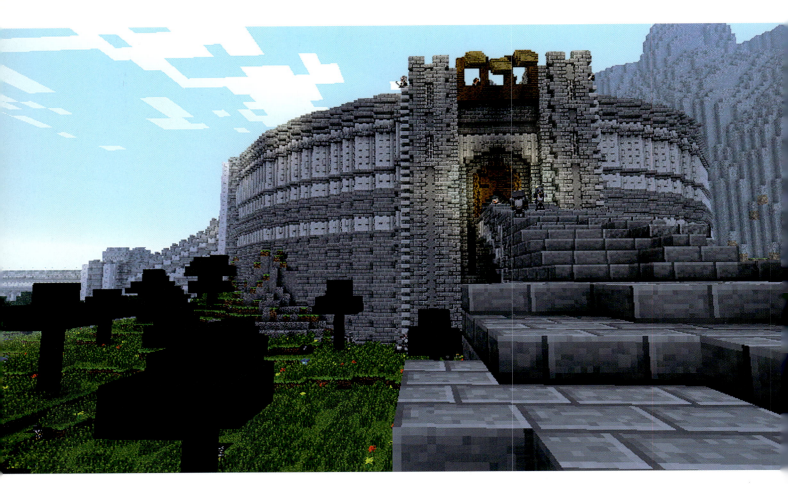

THE WIDE WORLD
OF PC MODS

We've always said that what you can do in Minecraft is limited only by your imagination, and while it's true that you can build just about anything you can think of in the regular game, there's another facet of Minecraft that takes the game and truly does turn it into whatever the human mind can come up with. They're called mods, short for modifications, and they are little bits of code written by fans just like yourself that add amazing new features or change Minecraft in unbelievable and super cool ways, such as turning your

character into a wizard, throwing hundreds of new weapons into the game, adding other characters and quests to go on or even silly/awesome stuff like letting you turn into a hamster! A hamster!

Unfortunately for those of you that play Minecraft on consoles exclusively, mods haven't made it to the console versions and, sadly, probably won't for a lot of reasons (mostly due to the operating systems not being built to handle the crazy things mods do to games). However, those that play on the PC or Mac can easily load up a few of these bad boys into their game, and even if you play on console, they're still great fun to take a peek at. Plus, since the game is only $25 on the PC, and it can run on just about any computer from the last 5 years, it might not be a bad thing to make the jump and start Crafting on the PC as well!

Either way, here's a little info on what kind of mods are out there, as well as a look at a few that really blow us away (sometimes quite literally).

ABOUT MODS

When someone makes a mod, they're actually going in and writing computer code to make temporary changes to the game, which then needs to be loaded into the game's regular code. Because of this, mods can vary greatly in all respects, from how many changes they make, to how big those changes are, to how big the files in the mod are and how they get loaded into the game's normal code.

There are almost as many types of mods as there are mods themselves (of which there are thousands), but most of them fit into one of these categories:

Utility mods: These are meant to be useful and are usually very small. They do things like add a better map to your interface, tell you the exact amount of daylight/night left, or make it easier to find friends. They also tend to work with other mods easily.

Small mods: Smaller mods usually tweak or add just one small thing or set of things. For instance Asgard Shield is a mod that adds shields, new weapons and the ability to guard to Minecraft, but leaves everything else the same. Playing with small mods usually doesn't feel all that different from the regular game, there's just a little more to do.

Big mods: As opposed to small mods, you'll notice when you load up a game with a big mod. They tend to change large parts of the game significantly, making it a mostly or entirely new experience. As an example, one such mod is the Tinkers' Construct, which takes the regular method of crafting tools and items through a Crafting Table and makes it much more complicated, adding multiple types of crafting stations, tables and forges and making players use Patterns and build each individual part of the tool they want. Another example is the Aether mod, which adds an entire new dimension in the sky.

Full conversion mods: Full conversion mods are big mods that are the most noticeable, because they change the game in huge ways, usually so much so that the objective when playing them is something new. This category includes mods like The Crafting Dead, which aims to turn the Minecraft world into a Zombie apocalypse wasteland. It includes guns, advanced Zombies and new systems for thirst, whether you are able to be seen or heard, temperature and even whether you're bleeding. Even cooler, it also adds in new specially generated maps that simulate the world of a Zombie apocalypse. Though you can (and should) build in The Crafting Dead, the goal is much more about surviving Zombie attacks and living on in a much harsher world than it is about mining and the like, making it a full conversion of the game.

Modpacks: The biggest of all, modpacks are groups of mods that have been put together by players and/ or mod creators in curated packages so that they all load together. These are the best place to start out when it comes to mods, as they are usually very easy to load, and they give you the chance to experience many of the best mods right away. Additionally, mods can be very picky about working together normally, but modpacks are specially put together so that they just work without you having to do much of anything.

It ain't hard to see why A Era do Futuro is so popular. Even the trees are different and amazing, as seen in this shot of the included Twilight Forest mod by wikispaces!

A ERA DO FUTURO
www.technicpack.net

One of the best and easiest ways to load up a modpack is to use a mod loader, which is a program that cuts out the need to open a bunch of folders and move files around (something you have to do for many mods). Of the mod loaders out there, the Technic Launcher is the most popular, and for good reason. Not only is it simple, cool-looking and very stable, it also includes some of the best mods and modpacks there are.

Of the Technic modpacks, A Era do Futuro is the most popular, and for good reason: it contains over 40 of the Minecraft world's most beloved mods. In a nutshell, it overhauls pretty much every facet of the game, including the biomes (with mod Extra Biomes XL), the mobs (Mo'Zombies, Mutant Creatures, Primitive Mobs and more), the weapons (Asgard Shield, Legend Gear, More Bows and more) and just about everything else. With A Era do Futuro, you'll be able to build amazing machines, fly to space, travel through a fantasy forest dimension and ever so much more, making it one of the best modpacks to wet your whistle with when starting out.

A typical idyllic floating island scene from an Aether world by gilded games. Don't fall off, now!

THE AETHER
bit.ly/TheAetherForum

The Aether mod adds a new dimension to your world that is the polar opposite of the Nether. The Aether is a sky dimension, and it keeps with that theme by including flying animals (Pigs with wings!), lots of cloud-based items and a very fluffy and light look and feel. It's also a huge challenge however, as it adds in three neat little Aether dungeons that have dangerous mobs and bosses in them, and each of which has a reward.

It's one of the more popular Minecraft mods out there, both for its look and for the fact that it's just very well done. As opposed to many mods, The Aether feels at once complete, complex and perfectly at home in the world of Minecraft, and though it does add a very big number of new items, block types and mobs, all of that stuff can only be picked up or seen in The Aether itself, meaning that the rest of your Minecraft world will stay the same. This makes it feel like just a really big update to the regular game, as opposed to mods that make Minecraft feel like a totally different game (though that's fun too!).

Agrarian Skies is chock full of some of the most popular mods that add new items and systems to your game. In just this shot alone you see new Barrels, a new type of Chest, a Half-Slab Furnace and a Sifting Table, used to get mineral materials and more from Dirt, Gravel, Sand and Dust (Dust!) blocks.

AGRARIAN SKIES
www.feed-the-beast.com

Mods are awesome: that, we think most everyone would agree on. However, since mods add so much new stuff and change up the game so extensively, it can be super overwhelming to fire one up and see all this new stuff you don't know how to mess with. Many mods come with little in-game Books that you can open up and read, but trying to remember all the things you read and switching back and forth between them and actually playing is pretty darn hard, even for the best Crafters.

That's why we suggest that, if you're looking to actually learn how to do some of the amazing things in mods like all of the Tinkers' mods, Thaumcraft, Thermal Expansion or Applied Energistics, check out the Agrarian Skies modpack. Actually a super, super modded version of Skyblock (see the Mini-Games section) and available on the FTB Launcher, Agrarian Skies puts you in a world where you have very little to start with, but all of the things you need to eventually build everything in the mods. It uses a very well-done and inventive questing system to teach you how to do a ton of the stuff in these mods by making them goals, and it does so in a way that's both hugely entertaining and also quite challenging. If we had to pick, Agrarian Skies would be our very favorite modpack of all.

Above: One addition people often overlook when it comes to mods is terrain generation. Attack of the B-Team has some great stuff when it comes to turning your basic landscape into something a bit more extreme. Bottom: If riding an Enderdragon isn't enough to get you downloading this mod, we don't know what will be. Unleash your inner Khaleesi, like BarracudaATA here!

ATTACK OF THE B-TEAM

www.technicpack.net

Wacky doesn't begin to describe this mod for lovers of the weird, the wacky and the just plain fun. Another Technic Launcher mod, Attack of the B-Team's website says that it "was designed with one thing in mind, crazy mad science! With the help of the B-Team we hand picked the wackiest mods we could find and shoved them all in a modpack for you guys."

In it you'll find all the best mods that have a strange twist to them, like the Hats mod which, as you might guess, adds a ton of hats for both you and mobs, or the Morph mod, which lets you turn into other creatures such as mobs. Combine that one with the Hamsterrific and Hamsters Forever mod, the awesome giant, exploding, purple-shooting dubstep gun from the Sainstpack, and a whole lot more, and you can see how Attack of the B-Team is one of the most fun, if most bizarre, modpacks that's yet been made.

Above: The new user interface for Crafting Dead shows you everything from your kill count, to how loud you're being to even how much blood you have left. Don't let that last one hit zero, by the way. Bottom: This Crafter is goin' at an updated and much stronger Crafting Dead Zombie with a good old fashioned chainsaw.

THE CRAFTING DEAD
bit.ly/CraftingDeadTechnic

Crafting Dead is, as the name might give you a slight hint about, a Minecraft mod based loosely on everyone's favorite zombie apocalypse TV show, *The Walking Dead.* As the creators say, it's also got a little *DayZ* thrown in there, and with the current popularity of that game plus the show, there's no better time to jump into Official Crafting Dead.

And don't expect this to just be Minecraft + a crapload of zombies; it is that (of course), but Official Crafting Dead also throws in a whole new set of survival and combat-related features such as a ton of new

weapons (guns!), new biomes and systems that tell you whether you're being too loud, too visible or are getting too thirsty. You can even fall and break your legs, which is weirdly awesome.

Above: The world of The Fellowship is huge, literally the entire size of Middle Earth as it is in the books and films, and it is dotted with awesome structures like this fort. Bottom: You'll have to figure out how to open the portal to the land of *Lord of the Rings* by exploring this world, and then it's game on!

THE FELLOWSHIP

bit.ly/FellowshipForum

Frankly, this is the *Lord of the Rings* experience we've been dreaming of in our most feverish, Gandalf-lovin' nerd dreams. This modpack is all about living in Middle Earth, and you can explore the whole realm, from Hobbiton all the way to fiery Mordor. The game is as off-rails as can be, meaning no one's sitting there forcing you to go kick Uruk Hai butt, and if you want to save the realm, you gotta step away from the elevensies table and get to it yourself.

This modpack is absolutely huge, with 42 separate mods included that run the gamut from the implementation of magic (the beloved Ars Magica

mod) to a new set of monsters to a whole adventuring system based on the monumental fantasy series. This is one of those mods that outright changes everything about your Minecraft experience, and it's not to be slept on by fantasy fans (read: pretty much everyone).

Yep: FTB Unleashed is super, super complicated, but that's half the fun! Using its systems, you can automate just about every part of Minecraft, if you know how.

FEED THE BEAST UNLEASHED
www.feed-the-beast.com

As they'll tell you on their site, Feed the Beast is a modder group that started out making a Skyblock challenge map (see the Mini-Games section), which they used mods to create. After a while, the maps they made and the mods required to use them got really complex, so they decided to start releasing modpacks so that it would be easier for everyone involved. This modpack has since been passed around simply for the quality of experiences it adds to a vanilla game, as its well-rounded inclusions feature everything from mods that turn you into a wizard to those that will allow you to add crazy new Redstone functions that were previously impossible.

Head to the page at the link to the left, and just look at everything that's included in this pack. A serious-builder's dream, Unleashed contains all the mods you could need to make just about any kind of structure, system, machine or other creation, plus some fun stuff like the ultra-cool Mystcraft (based on the game *Myst,* lets you create custom dimensions to travel to!). If you're looking for a way to spice up your game, and you're up for the challenge of building complex structures, FTB Unleashed is the be-all-end-all of builder packs.

Who wouldn't want Minecraft in space?! We know we do, and we know tdriling did when they built this excellent spacestation.

GALACTICRAFT
bit.ly/GalacticraftForum

Included in many modpacks (such as A Era do Futuro), Galacticraft deserves its own section because what it does is just so darn cool: it lets you build a rocketship and go to space! SPACE! In actuality, Galacticraft is a lot more than that, adding entire new systems and hundreds of new items and block-types to the game, all of which have a high-tech, sci-fi kind of theme to them.

The "space" you go to in Galacticraft is pretty awesome too, being basically three new dimensions that you can travel to and build in. These include the moon (no longer just a bunch of pixels hanging in the sky, but an actual place you can fly to and stand on!), the space around the earth (meant to be as if you're in orbit, and you can build space stations there) and Mars. If you fire this mod up and are lookin' to take a rocket up to see what you can find, however, make sure you bring a spacesuit, as even virtual space doesn't have a whole lot of air for your character to breathe!

(Though fine on its own, we'd suggest grabbing Galacticraft in Technic's Tekkit modpack, which is made to make Galacticraft even better by adding other complementary mods.)

Above: Hexxit not only adds new procedurally generated structures to come across in your world, it allows you to do some awesome new fantasy-themed builds of your own, like overload did here.

HEXXIT

www.technicpack.net

Like wizards and spells and trolls and all that wonderful fantasy stuff? Then you'll love Hexxit, the premier magic-based modpack and another excellent addition to the Technic Launcher. Similar to The Fellowship, but with the idea that you're creating your own adventure in a world no one's ever seen but you (as opposed to the world of Middle Earth).

Hexxit really changes the way you play Minecraft, not only because you're able to cast spells, build new weapons and fight all sorts of mythical and mystical new mobs, but also because it moves the focus of the game more heavily to exploration. The idea in Hexxit is that there are dungeons, towers and wrecked castles laying around the world, and as a wandering warrior, it's up to you to find, explore and, yes, loot the heck out of them. If exploring the landscape is your favorite part of the game, Hexxit makes that even better by turning it into a full-on adventure.

Pixelmon contains almost all of your favorite Pokémon, just wandering around and waiting to be captured.

PIXELMON

bit.ly/PixelmonOfficial
bit.ly/PixelmonTechnic

It's no secret that *Pokémon* is one of the most popular and long-lasting game series' of all time, so that the hardcore modding community for Minecraft has gone out and recreated *Pokémon* inside of their own game is no big shock to anyone. Pixelmon is just that modpack, and to answer your questions: Yes, there are Pokémon wandering around; yes, you can catch them; yes, you can fight them with trainers and other players; and yes, it all works.

Though you can just load this one up through the Feed the Beast launcher and play in your own world, we'd also suggest jumping on one of the official servers (just go to multiplayer instead of single player, and they're listed) where people have actually gone so far as to build functioning Pokémon Centers, gyms and even the Elite Four! Plus, you can show off your sick Mewtwo and find hundreds of other players to battle with. This one's a treat, whether you're a longtime *Pokémon* fan or just like the idea of a bunch of adorable battle creatures wandering around your Minecraft home.

HEROES OF MINECRAFT

With Minecraft being such a very popular game, and with so many incredible things having been done in the game, it's no surprise that there are a few Crafters out there whose skills and abilities make them special players of the game. We're talking about some seriously amazing Minecrafters, whether they're masters of Redstone, map builders extraordinaire, owners of popular servers, or just plain famous personalities in the game.

Though this list is far from comprehensive, here are some of the Minecrafters we love for their achievements in the game, which we think are so darn cool that they make these players Heroes of Minecraft.

To get the full effect here, you need to know that what looks like the ground is actually the wall. Yep: you're falling right now!

Another angle of the awesome bedroom level. Note: that bed is quite a lot bigger than most houses people build in the game.

BIGRE

Specialty: Creative maps, especially puzzle maps
Can be found at: bit.ly/bigremap

Bigre is a map creator best known for his wildly popular mini-game map called The Dropper, which features various highly decorated areas that players must fall through without hitting anything. In fact, The Dropper is by far the most downloaded map on the biggest Minecraft map repository (PlanetMinecraft.com), where it has been downloaded over 1 million times. In addition to The Dropper and its sequel, Bigre has also created a number of other mini-games, maps and even a resource pack. Though he's not quite as prolific or high profile as many of the others on this list, the importance of this map to the community and the creativity Bigre puts into their builds makes them one of our Minecraft Heroes.

A shot from CaptainSparklez's "Fallen Kingdom" music video, a parody of Coldplay's "Viva la Vida" done Minecraft style.

CAPTAINSPARKLEZ

Specialty: Let's Play Minecraft videos on YouTube, also MC related music videos

Can be found at:
YouTube- bit.ly/CaptainSparklezVideos
Twitter- bit.ly/CaptainSparklezTweets

Let's Play videos are the biggest things on YouTube right now (outside of music videos), with countless millions of views. What is a Let's Play? Essentially, they're simply recordings of people playing video games and chatting over them, and they're a whole lot of fun to watch. CaptainSparklez is an immensely popular Let's Play creator on the net, and his videos span everything from mod tests to mini-games and even parody music videos done up Minecraft style. Speaking of those music videos, CaptainSparkles currently holds the record for the three most-viewed Minecraft videos period (excluding the official trailer for the game), all of which are music videos. His most popular video "Revenge - A Minecraft Parody of Usher's DJ Got Us Fallin' in Love - Crafted Using Noteblocks" has over 136 million views, making it among the top 300 watched videos ever on YouTube.

Circleight is a master of color and mood, as you can see in this world that is somehow both dark and vibrant at once.

Few players build on the scale that Circleight does, yet her details are also among the game's best. Here we see her Divinus Concientia map.

CIRCLEIGHT

Specialty: Intensely creative and extremely large builds
Can be found at: bit.ly/CircleightMaps

If you ever want to show someone just how amazing Minecraft can be and just how insane the creations can get, Circleight's maps should be your first stop. This girl is a true artist, creating what are arguably the most gorgeous megabuilds of all time. She tends to work with lots and lots of rich colors on massive structures like temples and cathedrals, and she has not had a single map released that was anything short of beautiful. And when we say massive, we mean so dang massive that even on the PC version of the game set to load 16 chunks (which is huge), it's hard to load even one side of a Circleight structure at once. If you feel like checking out her thoroughly inventive and awe-inspiring builds, we'd suggest starting with the awesome Xenohasia building or the very well-done adventure map Desino City.

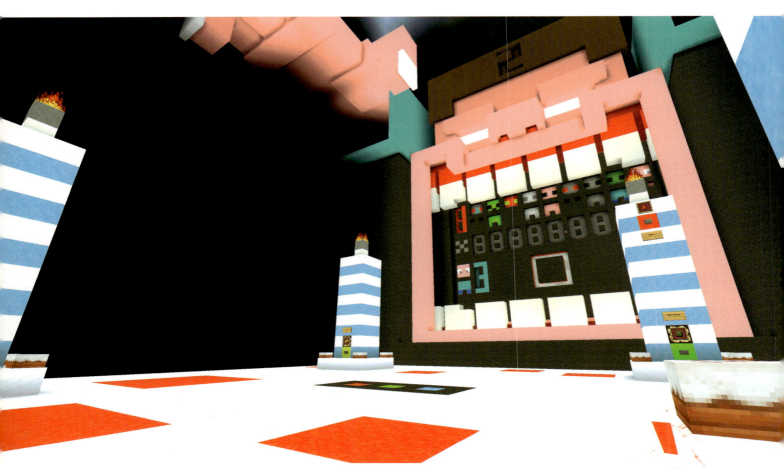

When it comes to imaginative mini-games, FVDisco takes the cake. In this level, however, the point is to keep mobs from taking your cake!

FVDISCO

Specialty: Redstone mad genius, mostly builds mini-games, created the oCd Texture Pack

Can be found at: Homepage- www.ocddisco.com
YouTube- bit.ly/FVDiscoYouTube
Twitter- bit.ly/FVDiscoTwitter
PlanetMinecraft- bit.ly/discoPMC

Being able to build working complex mechanisms with Redstone is impressive enough on its own, but Crafter FVDisco (aka disco_) goes far above and beyond when it comes to Redstone builds. Not only are his builds genius from an engineering standpoint, they're also made to be a heck of a lot of fun, almost always featuring a mini-game of some sort. Even more impressive, FVDisco is so very careful about what blocks are placed where that he has a style of building that is immediately recognizable, something few Crafters ever achieve. Part of disco's unique aesthetic comes from the oCd Texture Pack he created for his own builds, which is one of the cleanest, brightest and most fun texture packs available. Jump over to disco's PlanetMinecraft page and snag a few of his maps if you're looking for a little bit of mini-game fun that'll make you go, "Wow, how did he do this?!"

As leader of the MindCrack group, one of the most prestigious and awesome in the game, Guude sets up sessions like the Ultra Hardcore competition, which can be found on YouTube.

GUUDE/MINDCRACK

Specialty: Let's Play videos on YouTube, creator and leader of the MindCrack server

Can be found at: Homepage- www.mindcracklp.com
YouTube- bit.ly/GuudeYouTube
Twitter- bit.ly/GuudeTweets

MindCrack is a very special part of the Minecraft community. It's a group and a Minecraft server that often put out videos of gameplay on the server or with the group, which itself features many of the most popular Minecraft players in the world. This includes players SethBling, pauseunpause, kurtmac, BdoubleO100, Generikb, Etho, Nebris, Vechs and more, and it is run by the inimitable Guude. Essentially, Guude has created a group and a server where only the best of the best of the Minecraft world can get together and build and play, and they then release recordings of the amazing and hilarious things they get up to on their own YouTube channels. These videos are some of the most-watched on the website, and can feature everything from adventure map Let's Plays to highly competitive competitions, such as the long-running Ultra HardCore (UHC) contest which pits MindCrack members against each other in small groups, with the goal being to have your team survive the longest in a world where only Golden Apples can be used to heal. They're immensely fun to watch and often feature new mods, options and guest stars, such as when UHC 16 included a constantly shrinking world border and Mojang employee and Minecraft game developer Dinnerbone playing on a team.

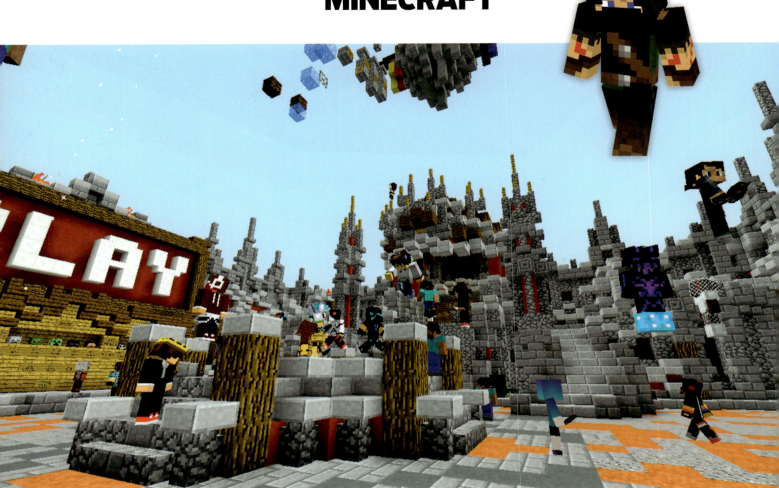

HYPIXEL

Specialty: Creators of very famous mini-game and adventure maps, popular server owners

Can be found at: Homepage- hypixel.net
YouTube- bit.ly/HypixelYouTube
Twitter- bit.ly/GuudeTweets
PlanetMinecraft- bit.ly/HypixelPMC

Hypixel is a true Minecraft building legend. Featuring two guys named Simon and Rezzus, Hypixel is a team that has created some of the most well-known and widely played mini-game and adventure maps in Minecraft history. Hypixel works with style and creative flair, coming up with inventive concepts and challenges and executing them beautifully, making games that are as fun as they are visually appealing. Their maps tend to also feature a ton of excellent Redstone mechanisms, such as the Gem Collector map which actually features a playable video game built inside of Minecraft. Hypixel is most well-known for two maps in particular: the gloomy and gorgeous Herobrine's Mansion adventure map, which features custom monsters and multiple boss fights on a map that actually has a story to play through and beat, and The Walls. The Walls is a PvP map that, through a stroke of genius, starts players in four corners of the map separated by massive walls. Eventually, the walls drop and the players must be prepared to combat each other to the death. The Walls is a true classic map, and it's so popular that you'll find it playable on a ton of Minecraft servers to this day, despite it being a year old. Hypixel also runs an excellent mini-game server themselves, which is almost always full of people and often holds giant contests. It's well worth a visit.

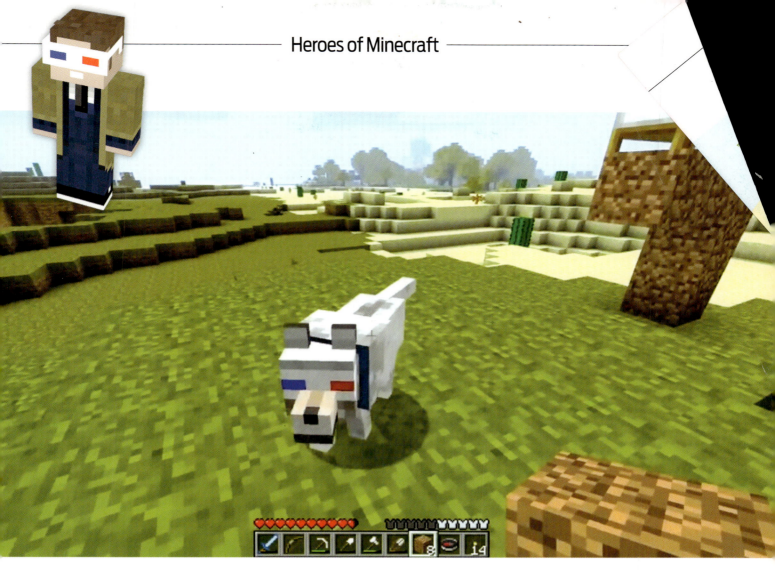

KURTJMAC

Specialty: Is walking to the Far Lands on YouTube, other Let's Play videos, Minecraft-related charity work

Can be found at: Homepage- farlandsorbust.com
YouTube- bit.ly/kurtjmacYouTube
Twitter- bit.ly/kurtjmacTwitter

Among our Minecraft Heroes, kurtjmac is a pretty unique dude. Unlike the rest, he isn't really known for his builds, for making maps or other downloadables or for running a server; he's known for his one-man (and dog!) journey from the spawn point to what is known as the Far Lands. These are essentially areas at the far edge of the Minecraft world where the algorithm that creates infinite Minecraft worlds essentially breaks down and stops working. They are insanely far from the spawn point, 12,550,821 blocks away in fact. It is calculated that walking to the Far Lands without cheating would take 820 hours (34 entire days and some hours), making it a hugely difficult task. Not to be deterred, kurtjmac has been walking since March 28, 2011 and has recorded every step of the way for YouTube (over 360 episodes so far). Along the way, kurt talks about life and things that interest him, and he even picked up a pet dog Wolfie, who has become massively popular in his own right. The Far Lands have actually been changed to no longer appear as of PC version 1.8, so kurt plays on an older version in order to keep up the quest. His vids are quite popular, and he has used this fame to raise hundreds of thousands of dollars for charity causes like Child's Play (which gets toys and games to kids in hospitals), making him a hero both in Minecraft and in real life.

MINECRAFT-PG5

Specialty: Redstone engineers, create everything from mini-games to useful tools

Can be found at: YouTube- bit.ly/MCPG5YouTube
Twitter- bit.ly/MCPG5Twitter
PlanetMinecraft- bit.ly/MCPG5PlanetMinecraft

Another crafter group, minecraft-pg5, or mcpg5 for short, is a team of "Redstone professionals" that have a bit of an edge on the rest of us when it comes to wiring up in Minecraft: they're actual electrical engineers! Using their actual engineering knowledge, these guys have created an outright ton of maps, making everything from adventures to parkour to mini-games to just cool little Redstone mechanisms. To give you an idea of how prolific these guys are at building: most big-time builders like SethBling and

Hypixel have 15-30 builds on . mcpg5 has 106. That's 3-7 more times than the average, and through their huge volume of builds, mcpg5 proves that just about anything you can think of can be done with Redstone, if you know what you're doing. If you're looking for some inspiration for your own Redstone builds, or some excellent builds to use to learn how to do certain Redstone tricks, you'll want to check these guys out ASAP.

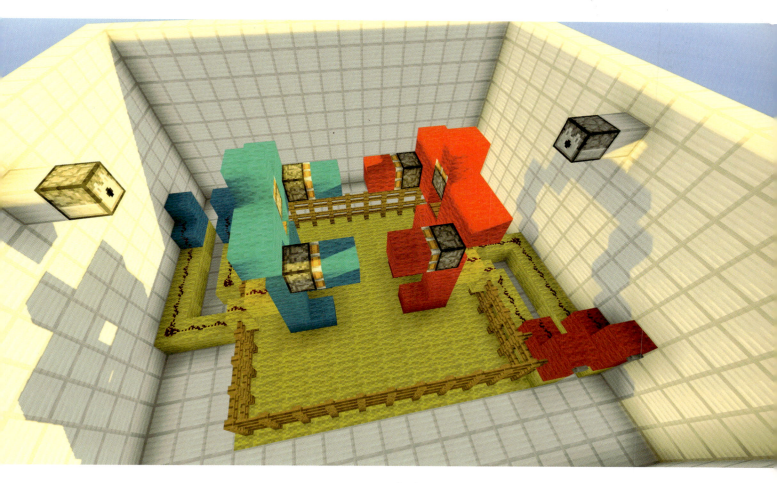

SETHBLING

Specialty: Reigning king of Redstone, Let's Play videos, map creator

Can be found at: Homepage- sethbling.com
YouTube- bit.ly/SethBlingYouTube
Twitter- bit.ly/SethBlingTwitter
PlanetMinecraft- bit.ly/SethBlingPMC

If Redstone had a pantheon of gods, it would include FVDisco, mcpg5 and the legendary SethBling. SethBling is one of the most well-known Minecraft players in general, a legend which began with his beloved maps such as the ubiquitous SkyGrid Survival Map (an insane grid of individual blocks floating in the sky), Super Craft Bros (Smash Brothers in Minecraft),

SethBling's Minecraft TNT Olympics and much more. Seth is one of the most active and visible members of the Minecraft community, posting on his Twitter and Facebook daily, as well as releasing YouTube and Twitch streaming videos of him doing everything from revealing awesome new Redstone creations (he built a Stargate portal that works not too long ago), playing mini-games and PvP with folks like his MindCrack pals, doing Let's Plays of other games and generally just having as much fun playing the game as he can. He's one of the most knowledgeable players of Minecraft there is, and he's always up to date with the most recent news and inventions, so follow him at his various outlets online to boost your MC know-how exponentially.

Sky is also known for his supa-cool music videos that feature some pretty dang awesome animation, not to mention singing.

SKYDOESMINECRAFT

Specialty: One of the top most Let's Play video creators, also makes parody songs about Minecraft

Can be found at: Homepage- skydoesminecraft.com
YouTube- bit.ly/SkyDoesYouTube
Twitter- bit.ly/SkyDoesTwitter

When it comes to entertaining Minecraft Channels, SkyDoesMinecraft might just take the cake. With over 10 million subscribers and nearly 2 billion views, Sky has the most popular Minecraft channel on YouTube, and considering how much Minecraft stuff there is on that site, that's saying a lot. Sky tends to do nicely produced Let's Play videos of various mods, mini-games and more that feature his charismatic voice-overs and each of which gets millions of views. He's a funny guy, and people absolutely love him, something that has led to his followers even getting their own name: the Sky Army. If you're new to the whole Let's Play phenomenon, SkyDoesMinecraft's channel is an excellent place to start out.

The Yogscast play Agrarian Skies! Two of our very most favoritest Minecraft things together in one glorious YouTube series.

THE YOGSCAST

Specialty: Hugely popular Minecraft YouTube channel for a group that does Let's Plays, parody songs and much more

Can be found at: Homepage- www.yogscast.com YouTube- bit.ly/YogsYouTube1 (there are many more Yogscast channels) Twitter- bit.ly/YogsTwitter

Oh, the Yogscast, we love you ever so dearly. While SkyDoesMinecraft might have the most subscribers, and CaptainSparklez might have the top three viewed Minecraft videos, there is no doubt that the biggest name in Minecraft right now is the Yogscast. Featuring over a dozen members, each of whom has a following of their own, the Yogscast is a true Internet phenomenon. Beginning in 2008 with primary members Simon and Lewis, Yogscast began as a *World of Warcraft* guild which released YouTube videos showing how to do things in the game. Eventually, Simon and Lewis expanded to Minecraft videos, which became immensely popular, especially in their home country of the UK. When it comes to their videos, these guys do just about everything from mod spotlights to parody songs to PvP to even a sort-of sitcom done inside of Minecraft with various members playing characters. They are hilarious, very British and muchly deserving of the huge amounts of attention they get. If we had to suggest anyone's Minecraft videos, these are the guys we'd send you to without any hesitation.